LEARNING
WORK

Critical Studies in Education and Culture Series

Critical Pedagogy and Cultural Power
David Livingstone and Contributors

Education and the American Dream: Conservatives, Liberals and Radicals Debate the Future of Education
Harvey Holtz and Associates

Education and the Welfare State: A Crisis in Capitalism and Democracy
H. Svi Shapiro

Education under Seige: The Conservative, Liberal and Radical Debate over Schooling
Stanley Aronowitz and Henry A. Giroux

Literacy: Reading the Word and the World
Paulo Freire and Donaldo Macedo

The Moral and Spiritual Crisis in Education: A Curriculum for Justice and Compassion
David Purpel

The Politics of Education: Culture, Power and Liberation
Paulo Freire

Popular Culture, Schooling and the Language of Everyday Life
Henry A Giroux and Roger I. Simon

Teachers As Intellectuals: Toward a Critical Pedagogy of Learning
Henry A. Giroux

Women Teaching for Change: Gender, Class and Power
Kathleen Weiler

Between Capitalism and Democracy: Educational Policy and the Crisis of the Welfare State
Svi Shapiro

Critical Psychology and Pedagogy: Interpretation of the Personal World
Edmund Sullivan

Pedagogy and the Struggle for Voice
Catherine E. Walsh

LEARNING WORK

A CRITICAL PEDAGOGY OF WORK EDUCATION

ROGER I. SIMON,
DON DIPPO,
AND ARLEEN SCHENKE

CRITICAL STUDIES IN EDUCATION AND CULTURE SERIES

EDITED BY HENRY A. GIROUX AND PAULO FREIRE

Bergin & Garvey
New York • Westport, Connecticut • London

Library of Congress Cataloging-in-Publication Data

Simon, Roger I.
   Learning work : a critical pedagogy of work education / Roger I.
Simon, Don Dippo, Arleen Schenke.
      p.   cm.—(Critical studies in education and culture series)
   Includes bibliographical references and index.
   ISBN 0–89789–237–2 (alk. paper). — ISBN 0–89789–240–2 (pbk. :
alk. paper)
      1. Education, Cooperative—Canada.   2. Career education—Canada.
I. Dippo, Donald A., 1950–   II. Schenke, Arleen.   III. Title.
LB1029.C6S525   1991
370.11′3′0971—dc20   90–49196

British Library Cataloguing in Publication Data is available.

Library of Congress Catalog Card Number: 90–49196
ISBN: 0–89789–237–2 (hb.)
       0–89789–240–2 (pb.)

First published in 1991

Bergin & Garvey, One Madison Avenue, New York, NY 10010
An imprint of Greenwood Publishing Group, Inc.

Printed in the United States of America

∞

The paper used in this book complies with the
Permanent Paper Standard issued by the National
Information Standards Organization (Z39.48–1984).

10 9 8 7 6 5 4 3 2 1

To Studs Terkel
who taught us so much about how to listen
and hear the expression of human dignity
upon which all productive work is founded

Contents

Preface   ix

Series Introduction: Reading Work Education
    as the Practice of Theory *by Henry A. Giroux*   xiii

Part I   **Introduction**

1   Work Education and Critical Pedagogy   3

2   Strategies for Critical Reflection in Work
       Education   13

Part II   **Exploring Technical Relations**

3   Working Knowledge: What It Takes to Do
       the Job   27

4   Skills and Work Design   45

5   Teachers Working with Employers:
       Developing the Learning Potential of
       Work Sites   57

Part III   **Exploring Social Relations**

6   Working Through Social Relations   75

7   Occupational Health and Safety: A Critical
       Look   95

8   Time On and Off the Job: The Interrelation of
       Work, Desire, and Leisure   113

9   Unions: Solving Problems by Sticking
       Together   127

Part IV   Exploring Work as an Exchange Relation

10   Self-Assessment: Changing Circumstances,
       Changing Selves   149

11   Speaking Out about Pay   165

12   Getting a Job   175

13   Future Work   185

       Index   197

Preface

What is work education? In its most general sense, work education is a practice that emphasizes the development of knowledge, skills, and attitudes that relate to a student's future participation within the economic sector of one's community and nation. In practice, such intentions become manifest in a considerable variety of program forms including career exploration, world of work, adult re-training, work transition, and high school and college work-study courses that combine alternating periods of time in schools and workplaces.

During the last decade there has been a world-wide movement to establish work education as a central component of public schooling and community-based "life skills" retraining programs. The establishment of work education has been motivated by a variety of concerns, including lowering school drop-out rates, helping students define a "career," helping students gain a sense of pride and accomplishment, and developing a competent and reliable supply of labor for community economic enterprise. With a manifold sense of purpose, work education programs have become a feature of a vast number of school districts and community service agencies not only in Canada and the United States, but in Britain and Australia as well.

However, as school districts rush to establish such programs, new questions are being asked as to how work education can be justified within a project of public schooling. Representatives of community agencies have also been debating how to confront the contradictions they at times feel between serving community economic interests and the educational needs of their clients. Such discussions signal the rekindling of an old debate regarding the relative balance between education and training both in public schools and community adult education. As both teachers and community-based educators resist turning their programs into training centers for existing corporate interests, concerns have arisen over how work education may proceed in a way that provides students with an understanding of "the realities" of life in the job market and at work, while helping them to increase their effective participation in determining the practices that will define their working lives. *Learning Work: A Critical Pedagogy of Work Education* directly addresses this concern. Through discussions of teaching practice and actual lesson suggestions we attempt to clarify how the viewpoint of a "critical pedagogy" can be used to develop a clear and principled practice of work education that directly addresses this concern.

We have assumed a multiple audience for this book. It will be of interest to teachers working in a variety of forms of work education programs, particularly programs that emphasize experiential components such as work-study or cooperative education. Community-based educators working in adult "life skills," "drop back," retraining, and literacy programs will also find many practical suggestions as well as a programmatic orientation for their work. However, there is a third, and equally important audience we have intended to address in our text: those educators and academics who have consistently complained about the lack of practical examples and overt concern for questions of teaching and learning in the literature which, over the last decade, has come to be referenced by the term "critical pedagogy and cultural studies." In our introduction, we provide a brief discussion of how we understand the project of a critical pedagogy and how it relates to work education. However, in this book we have emphasized questions of educational practice over abstract conceptualizations about practice. There is much theory in this book, but readers will find it encoded in the lesson suggestions and teaching notes that make up most of the following pages. Nevertheless, it is important to emphasize that this book could not have been written without our own participation in what is too often referred to as "academic abstractions," that is, the conceptual discussions of education as a form of cultural politics and the questions of power/ knowledge such discussions generate.

This book has been a long time coming. It began as part of an extended ethnographic research project on the production of work identities. Many examples in this book have been drawn from interviews and classroom observations compiled during our research in a cross-section of urban, suburban, and rural high schools in southern Ontario. While this research was crucial to our understanding of the problems and challenges of work education, we have not provided methodological details of this study here and the book should not be construed as a research report. The substance of this book reflects who we are and where we work. There is a definite Canadian (or at least an English-speaking southern Ontarian) character to the text. However, the majority of suggestions offered in this book can be used in different national contexts with small modification. Those lesson suggestions that do emphasize particular Canadian social contexts should be read for what they display as a particular approach, which can be adapted to local histories and economic realities.

Many friends and colleagues have contributed to this book. It could not have been written without the encouragement and labor of Jeff Piker. Jeff was central to the formation of the text and his draft contributions were invaluable in helping spur the constant process of revision. Many times it was his energy and enthusiasm that kept us going. Matt Sanger researched and wrote draft material for the chapter on unions. Alison Griffith provided analyses of research data which influenced the formation of many of the chapters. Diane Gérin-Lajoie provided an analysis that was helpful in drafting a portion of the chapter on social relations. Sam Serrano contributed useful commentary on draft material, and bravely tried out lesson suggestions in his own classroom. Many thanks also to Peter Phelan, Joan Ellis, and Danny Panzer for their comments and advice. Thanks also to Michael Chervin for a wonderful detailed edit of the introduction, and to Gael Tickner and Jo-Anne Hannah for comments on various aspects of draft material. Special thanks to Carol Broome, who spent many hours typing interview transcripts. This book is based on work supported by the Social Sciences and Humanities Research Council of Canada.[1]

NOTE

1. Under project numbers 410–81–0906, 410–83–0770, and 410–84–0109.

Series Introduction: Reading Work Education as the Practice of Theory

The relationship between work and schooling has long been the subject of theoretical and political analyses in both North America and elsewhere. Not surprisingly, the ideological contours that have been generated in order to define the "work" experience for countless numbers of students do not fall neatly into traditional political parameters. For example, various groups of progressive educators have long argued that schools should provide all students with the work skills they will need to function in the larger economy. On the other hand, a noticeable number of radical critics have argued that work education involves what has been called "tracking" in the United States and "streaming" in Canada—a process that functions, in terms of class, gender, or race, to largely prepare students for low-skill, dead-end jobs. More conservative analyses have criticized the nature of work education while supporting the larger goal of educating students for the workplace as one of the primary tasks of schooling. Such analyses have been more inclined to fault schools for simply not providing students with the necessary attitudes, knowledge, and skills to fulfill successfully their future participation in the world of work. Of primary concern has been the role of the school in fostering character traits and dispositions that will produce workers who will value tradition and respect the virtues of the worksite such as obedience, punctuality, compliance, and deference to authority. While all of these issues are central to any discourse *about* work education, they too often operate at a level of abstraction that fails to produce a pedagogy *for* work education. Hence, the great majority of these positions speak to and for students engaged in work education, but they rarely ever allow students to speak from the specificity of their own experiences; that is, from those places, practices, and spaces that frame their lives in particular ways. Within the dominant discourses on work education, children are positioned in a language that speaks for them rather than with them. Generally missing from these accounts are any analyses of how student identities are shaped in relation to the specificity of work education, and what implications this might have for expanding the theoretical and practical insights necessary for developing a pedagogy of work experience that is both concrete and transformative.

This should not suggest that work education programs have not been organized by educators to deal with the shifting demands for labor that have come to characterize most of the industrialized Western countries. Work education has, in some cases, become the new panacea for addressing the economic, political, and cultural crises that are threatening the political and economic stability of a large number of industrial nations. Rising levels of unemployment, lack of adequately trained workers for the increasing low-end service sectors of the economy, high dropout rates, and the changing cultural and demographic nature of the work force, have put the issue of work education high on the agenda of educational reform. The grim irony is that the theoretical models that frequently underpin these programs have a tendency to undermine whatever emancipatory potential they may have. Functional in nature and limited in vision, many educators and policymakers completely disregard how the pedagogical practices at work in these programs position students within shifting and often contradictory sets of experiences; and yet such experiences are integral to how students construct their senses of self and their relationships to others and to the world around them.

Learning Work is an important book both because it engages a broad range of debates and problems that have taken place around work education, and because it employs the term "practice" in a highly innovative and important way. Practice is used by Simon, Dippo, and Schenke to challenge the conventional manner in which theory and practice are understood by many educators, especially with respect to the relationship between the two. Practice, in this book, rewrites its relationship to theory in a dual sense. First, it "interrupts" the alleged autonomy of theory as merely a conceptual or abstract representational system by making visible the practices that construct theory, and by illuminating how theory can only be understood as a practice produced by the circumstances that structure its problems, possibilities, and inadequacies. Second, theory is not seen as the center of educational work, then assigning practice a marginal and secondary role. Practice is not romanticized as a sphere activity where truth, insight, and virtue automatically reveal themselves in experiential terms.

For the authors of *Learning Work*, critical pedagogy is important and potentially transformative to the degree that it re-invents theory as a practice rooted in self-reflection and as a critical awareness of its own historical and social formation. As part of a broader pedagogy of work experience, the authors illuminate this in a number of ways. First, the practice of theory in this book is grounded in both a recognition of its own partiality and a commitment to a radical democratic project. That is, practice, in this case, makes explicit the moral and political aims presupposed in the social relations that it structures as part of a broader attempt to deepen the possibilities for human dignity and democratic public life. Second, the authors rupture the binary opposition of theory and practice, while simultaneously challenging facile claims to an un-problematic cause and effect relationship between the two. Third, *Learning Work* makes clear that theory *as* a form of practice does not operate from the margins of a transformative critical pedagogy, but as a central and mutually constitutive aspect of a cultural politics that refigures the very problematic that constructs the history, meaning, and possibilities of work education.

Learning Work takes up the issue of a critical practice of work education as a basis for teachers, administrators, students, and others to rethink the most fundamental theoretical assumptions that render work education meaningful as both a critical pedagogy and as a cultural politics deeply implicated in the construction of citizens who will eventually occupy one of the most important public spheres in society. Practice in this sense becomes a basis for theorizing from a set of experiences, organized through the familiar ground of the particular, specific, and immediate.

By emphasizing the practice of a critical theory of work education, the authors have neither underplayed the importance of theoretical consid-erations, nor overemphasized the importance of experience in shaping work education. Instead, they have provided and privileged a set of pedagogical practices as a basis for teachers and other cultural workers to examine the diverse connections and complex conditions of work education that always necessitate a critical attentiveness to theoretical considerations and interventions.

The practices taken up in *Learning Work* serve as a brilliant attempt to make work education pragmatic and problematic—a practice that pre-supposes, affirms, and ruptures the often contradictory and shifting relationships between schooling as a form of social and moral discourse and the effects it has in either extending or undermining the capacities and competencies that students need to function as both workers and citizens in the twenty-first century. Work education, as it is presented by the authors, is not a master narrative for ethnographic research, critical pedagogy, or educational policy. On the contrary, while pointing to the importance of these issues, it engages rather than ignores how they are taken up or given expression within a particular historical context and cultural location. *Learning Work* in this sense serves to demonstrate how critical pedagogy is practiced as a form of cultural politics that legitimates itself less through a series of reasoned abstractions than within a set of concrete practices. Practice in this sense becomes a form of writing, an act of cultural production that both produces and carries out the script it creates as it unfolds through the shifting contours of representation, power, and place that configure the relations between teachers, students, homes, workplaces, and daily life.

Learning Work is a book that is practical, accessible, and informative. This is a book that will surely animate a lively debate among a broad public over the meaning, purpose, and practice of work education. It serves as a striking example of how complex theoretical issues can manifest themelves in a discourse of practice that refuses both dogmatic reductionism and abstract reification. This is also one of the first books within the field of critical pedagogy that combines the language of critique and hope within a project of possibility that presupposes in its practice the grounds for a more just and humane notion of work, schooling, and society.

Henry A. Giroux

I

Introduction

1

Work Education and Critical Pedagogy

The question of how and to what extent curriculum and teaching in schools should be linked to the requirements of a local or national economy is of concern to youth, families, teachers, businesses, labor organizations, and government. Such concerns are being addressed through school programs that claim to prepare people for "successful" and "productive" participation in the working life of the community and the nation. This is an issue whose educational importance is obvious. Yet in moving from the rhetoric of success and productivity to the realities of classroom practice, we need to acknowledge the complexity behind the inevitable task of interpreting what is meant by "successful" and "productive" participation. What range of possible answers to this question exists? What social interests are served by different answers? What answers are being heard and by whom? Given different versions of what constitutes adequate preparation for working life, how will our commitments as educators help us to decide what to do in our classrooms?

This book is intended to serve as a resource for teachers struggling with these questions. Through discussions of teaching practice and actual lessons we offer suggestions on how the project of a critical pedagogy can be used to develop a clear and principled practice of work education.

Our starting point acknowledges that education is not a neutral enterprise. Schools are places where a sense of identity, place, and worth is both informed and contested. This is a process that happens within the daily, concrete relations among staff and students, relations that affect the organization and regulation of what knowledge is to be made available and what meanings will be produced within the encounter of "going to school." Thus, how we do schooling really matters. It influences the way different people will answer questions such as: What knowledge is of most worth? What does it mean to know something? How might we construct useful or truthful representations of ourselves, others, and our physical and social environments? What modes of living are to be considered of value? In what direction should we desire? How might our efforts be directed, to adapting to the world "as it is" or to considering what would have to be done for things to be otherwise?

From this discussion we can see that the knowledge made available and the meanings produced within schooling are important events in our society for, at least in part, they define what we take to be our "horizon of possibility." The fact that what happens in schools influences our horizon of possibility gives what teachers and students actually do together a particular social significance. It means that schools are places within which a form of "cultural politics" happens. At first glance, this assertion may seem awkward and strange. However, if we consider politics as designating that process through which members of a group, community, or nation decide on ways they will live their common life together, the meaning of schools as a site of cultural politics becomes clearer. Certainly it is a form of politics when we are engaged in a process (and as teachers we are) that results in certain competencies and capacities being nominated as worthy of encouragement and development. And certainly it is a form of politics when we help construct an imagination that delimits the range of social forms within which we expect people to realize their capacities.[1]

It is our assumption that to develop an adequate conception of work education, one that will be coherent and capable of delivering on its promise to help prepare people for "successful" and "productive" working lives, we must be clear as to the cultural politics that will guide our pedagogy. This perhaps then signals the most significant contribution this book can make. While teachers will find many practical ideas that can be adapted for use in various forms of schooling for work in both high schools and community colleges, what is central to our efforts here is the clarification of a conception of work education organized within the frame of an explicit cultural politics. The broad outline of this politics and its realization as a critical pedagogy has been discussed elsewhere.[2] The aim of the rest of this introduction is to situate our approach to work education within the domain of critical pedagogy.

THE ONGOING POLICY DEBATE

In order to understand the distinctive character of our concept of work education it is helpful to first consider some earlier formulations of how schools could be linked to the economy. These formulations were attempts to provide specific directions for incorporating work-related issues into the curriculum. In the late 1800s a debate raged over the purpose and substance of vocational education. This debate can be characterized as a conflict between two views about the relationship between education and work, embedded in a larger framework of assumptions about the role of schools in serving society. One represents an instrumental view that schools are places committed to efforts for increasing social and economic efficiency; the other represents a pedagogic view that schooling is a process within which personal and social growth should be enhanced.

The social efficiency view is closely associated with David Snedden, then commissioner of education for the Commonwealth of Massachusetts and a leading advocate of segregated vocational schools. He argued in favor of programs to train students in specific vocational skills. He wrote: "The controlling purpose of vocational education is to produce fairly definite forms of skill and power which shall enable the learner to become a successful producer of a valuable service."[3] From an instrumental view, vocational curriculum was intended to provide students with specific job skills, behaviors, values, and attitudes to create a "properly" skilled and socialized work force.

One of the most articulate voices opposed to the idea of schooling as job-skills training was that of John Dewey, who suggested that such programs were inappropriate for any school system in that they take the interests of students and make them subservient to the interests of employers. He argued instead for a broader vision of work education which took as its primary objective

the development of such intelligence, initiative, ingenuity, and capacity as shall make workers as far as possible, masters of their own industrial fate. . . . The kind of vocational education in which I am interested is not one which will "adapt" workers to the existing industrial regime . . . but one which will alter the existing industrial system and ultimately transform it.[4]

For Dewey, a work curriculum should provide an education with broad social meaning aimed at transforming society and the organization of work within it to reflect participative, democratic values.

For almost 100 years the debate as to how to characterize the central purpose and method of schooling for work has centered on this distinction between training and education. This debate is still very much alive. In recent years, first in the wake of widespread youth unemployment and now in the context of an increasingly pervasive rhetoric that asserts the necessity of developing a globally competitive labor force, priority is again being given to the questions of how to incorporate work-related issues and competencies into the curriculum.

The voices advocating a training approach are as loud and as clear as ever. However, Snedden's original vision has shifted somewhat. Instead of emphasizing specific job-skills training, what is being increasingly advocated are generic "basic," "life," and "employability" skills. These are characteristics employers seem to think will help preserve the flexibility necessary to adapt to quickly changing competitive markets. While the emphasis has shifted, the important point here is the continuity of an approach that emphasizes the production, organization and regulation of human capacities to fit the existing social and technical relations and material conditions of the workplace.

Are there voices for education in this current milieu? There are, and they are coming from educators who continue to view public education as requiring schools that prepare people, not simply for employment, but rather, for participation in democratic communal life of which the workplace is a part. This vision for schools is consciously being articulated in response to constricted schooling agendas that emphasize individual, technical, and narrow economic interests.

Within the literature on education, the "education or training" debate is continuing in new and revitalized forms. In schools, however, the debate is muted by the fact that educational policymakers have insisted on defining schools as places within which students should be instrumentally prepared to meet both existing and projected economic requirements. This has left some teachers and administrators wondering how they could still reclaim the valued ground that schools have a role to play in developing forms of critical citizenship, while at the same time helping students gain the knowledge and skills needed to participate in the social relations of the economy. Our book is intended to address such educators. Rather than dichotomize education and training, what we are attempting to do is reformulate the relation between them in the service of helping people expand the range of possibilities through which they may define their working lives. It is for these reasons that we ask what it would mean both to learn about work and to learn how to do it.

THINKING ABOUT WORK—SUBSTANTIVE ISSUES FOR A WORK EDUCATION

Developing a program of work education that challenges the dominant instrumental understanding of the relation of schooling and the economy requires a conceptual framework that will allow us to take up the study of work. A basic issue in defining how a pedagogical approach to work education might be developed centers on how the concept of work may be characterized. What should be the starting assumptions about the nature of work?

One common approach to work education is founded on the assumption that in order to be relevant across a range of occupations it is necessary to abstract work from any particular occupational context.[5] This results in taking up the study of work "in general," which in effect means taking up nobody's work. Within this book we take the view that there is no such thing as work "in general"—that is, work that can be understood apart from its context and studied as a generic theme. Rather, work is always contextual and specific. This need not, however, lead to a narrow, technical concept of work education (as training). As an alternative we begin with a framework for understanding the structures and processes that organize practices and conditions in the workplace. This is an educational approach aimed at understanding the particular character of working while recognizing that all work is organized within historical and contemporary forms and relations of power.

The framework we propose requires an understanding of the particular character of working as an exchange relation within which manual and intellectual labor is commodified and exchanged for goods such as wages, food and shelter, or remuneration. Such exchange relations are constituted within either implicitly or explicitly codified contractual relationships. The terms of reference of such an exchange are often made evident in such forms as salary schedules, wage rates, bonus and incentive systems, stock-option plans, and so forth. Furthermore, such exchange relations are always simultaneously organized within both historically constituted technical and social relations of production. When we speak of technical relations we are referring to the tools, machines, technology, processes, work flow, and technical knowledge used in the production of goods or provision of services. Social relations, however, refer to the relations of workers to each other and to management. They would include the division of labor, the structures of authority, race, and gender relations.

The curriculum approach and lesson suggestions within this book focus on the interrelations among the three basic concepts of exchange, technical, and social relations. Such relations provide one way of recognizing the socially and politically constructed features of work. Emphasizing the historical, socially defined character of the work that people do enables us to recognize and clarify how the organization of work in society is neither natural or inevitable. This then allows us to emphasize teaching that helps students imagine, consider, and judge a variety of possibilities for how work may be accomplished.

DISTINGUISHING OUR APPROACH FROM CONTEMPORARY APPROACHES TO WORK EDUCATION

How do existing approaches to work education align themselves in relation to this characterization of the particular character of working?

We have found four common emphases in work education programs. Each can be discussed in terms of the relative emphases on the exchange character of work, the technical relations that organize and define tasks, and the social relations that constitute the organizational and interpersonal aspects of work.

1. helping students make "career choices," as in programs of career development (this approach emphasizes the exchange relation itself)
2. helping students develop the ability to get and keep a job, as in work and employability skills training (this approach emphasizes both social relations and the exchange relation)
3. providing students with a non-school environment and set of challenges in the hope that these will be beneficial to the maturation process, as in programs for students labelled "underachieving" or with attendance or discipline problems (this approach emphasizes both social and technical relations)
4. providing students with the opportunity to develop and learn new technical skills, as in traditional vocational programs (this approach emphasizes primarily technical relations)

The popularity and currency of these approaches fluctuate in relation to the debates over what should be done in the face of changing economic and social conditions. As we try to make evident in the following chapter, our approach encourages an understanding of the historical, cultural, and economic character of work as an exchange relation. Further, it asks students to consider how both the requirements and the opportunities of work in any particular workplace must be understood as integrally connected.

Our commitment is to enhance the ability of students to increase their effective participation in determining the practices that define their working lives. This is not necessarily a problem for individuals with individual solutions. Thus our approach is not limited, for example, to discussions of how individual occupational mobility might be enhanced. To do so would only be to pit people against each other instead of encouraging collective strategies to address shared problems that may require changing the social forms that define work possibilities, rather than simply competing for the positions within existing forms. We realize that potential solutions to such increased participation may require individual or collective forms of action. Furthermore, such goals may involve people in forms of social struggle. Such struggles must always be understood as taking place on particular historical terms. Thus work must be understood as a particular wage-labor exchange constituted on historical grounds with respect to the social and technical relations of production.

It must be made clear that this does not mean that our approach is unconcerned with the importance of teaching technical skills or the knowledge needed to get a job and keep one. Neither is our interest in irresponsibly sowing the seeds of disorder in relations between employers and employees. At the same time we do not wish to pull back from our commitment to a form of education that can enable people to act with a sense of hope and possibility in their lives.

JUSTIFYING THIS APPROACH IN OUR SCHOOLS

It should be clear that we are offering a particular approach to work education that encompasses both training *and* education. Furthermore it should be clear that we see that the trend of much current discussion ignores educational considerations to the exclusive emphasis on training functions. Our work herein is meant not only to provide some practical ideas for teaching work education but to add a "counter-discourse" as well to what is too quickly becoming the dominant voice in discussions of how to design and implement various versions of work education. Our intent is to argue for the establishment of a critical pedagogy of work education in our schools. A currently overlooked purpose for schooling is to provide a public sphere within which taken-for-granted, dominant modes of thought can be understood, debated, contested, and challenged through alternative conceptions of what it means to educate for both current and future visions of communal life.

When we begin thinking of schools in this way we can begin to understand both their singular importance and their inter-connectedness with other sites in our society within which a future sense of the possibility of our common life together is constituted. Identity formation is always taking place in families, workplaces, youth cultures, and schools. These sites act as "cultural technologies," producing a sense of what people think and feel is desirable and possible.[6] This identity formation process takes place in and through the encounters with people and events within these multiple sites. Such encounters often close down possibilities because we too readily and uncritically accept what presents itself as obvious and given. A pedagogy of possibility employed in any of these sites would have to contest this narrowing process.

For this reason, "experience," whether in one's home, work, neighborhood, or school, cannot be simply taken for granted. We must avoid the conservatism inherent in only confirming what people already know. Experience should never be celebrated uncritically. School is a place within which to explore the problematic character of experience

not [as] something obvious that speaks for itself, but rather as an understanding that is constructed as a particular interpretation of a specific engagement with material and people over time. It is on this basis that we argue that work education, by placing students in work situations, creates an occasion in which students necessarily confront ideas, terms, procedures, relations, and feelings in order to make sense of their presence in the workplace. How students do this—how they accomplish experience—depends in part on the beliefs, ideas, assumptions, and values they bring with them, but also on the context and content of reflection and analysis that we may be able to provide in work education programs.[7]

Schools can be and need to be sites that allow us the time and space to rethink our understanding of the way our world works, what made it that way, and what continues to reproduce the current state of affairs. What we as teachers can offer are concepts and a language that would help students interpret work-related situations and relations in the service of enhancing their ability to effectively participate in the determination of their working lives. We can provide an opportunity for students to engage new ideas and frameworks that challenge their taken-for-granted ways of thinking and help them voice, critically reflect on, and take more pride in alternative needs, desires, and possibilities. This, we assert, is basic to our responsibilities as educators.

OUR VIEW OF TEACHING AND LEARNING—WORKING ON AND WORKING WITH EXPERIENCE

The above discussion implies a view of teaching and learning that makes the constitution of experience central to work education. For this reason our version of work education does not simply mean providing students with what we take to be the right way to understand the work world. Neither is it simply a matter of imparting instrumentally useful knowledge. Rather, one must be able to help students to work both with and on their experiences in order to deepen their sense of how the existing requirements of the work world have been shaped and how such requirements might be altered and the consequent possibilities expanded.

What is the meaning of the distinction between *working with* and *working on* experience? Each of these must be understood in connection with the basic pedagogical task: that of setting the analytical categories of difference, similarity, contradiction, and historicity into relation with those commonsense understandings that are the basis for the experiences of pleasure, competence, and identity at work. That is, basic to the approach detailed in the lesson suggestions within this book is the use of a set of strategies for defining possibilities of student inquiry. Posing questions regarding the existence of similarity and difference among and within different views of common sense; setting up questions about the contradictory nature of many of our common understandings of working; and posing questions regarding the social origins of taken-for-granted everyday life situations are all methods within which students may find a starting point for the critical exploration of working. While such methods proceed from individual understandings, our approach is committed to developing understandings of shared problems rather than individual coping mechanisms. Thus the notions of difference, similarity, contradiction and historicity must be addressed at both individual and collective levels.

The agenda for inquiry sketched above can be accomplished within two approaches: *working on* and *working with* experience. As a particular mode of inquiry, *working on* is aimed at showing how work experience is a form of knowledge produced within a context of existing knowledge and practices. The task is to develop insights into how one's own experience and the experiences reported by others may be studied as situated knowledge claims and understood as provisional and contingent. As will be illustrated in the lesson suggestions to follow, whether students are studying texts that report how workers understand their jobs, interviewing workers on a job site, or examining their own personal work journals which record their daily work experience, "working on experience" is aimed at examining the processes that link the production of personal knowledge with the shared meanings, understandings and material conditions that characterize a work site. When inquiry into relations of difference, similarity, contradiction, and historicity are applied in such studies, they open up the possibility for understanding the workplace as a socially defined space within which neither custom nor values need be taken for granted or go unquestioned.

In contrast, *working with* experience is an attempt to explore how one's work experience is linked to the experiences of others in other places and in other times. What is emphasized in such study is that the contingent conditions implicated in work experiences are organized and regulated within ongoing social arrangements that have given shape to the way working has been accomplished in our society. This mode of inquiry requires helping students to understand how their experiences are linked to those of others situated differently by virtue of their social class, gender, race, age, geographical, and historical location. Such links will not only stress unifying commonalties among people. Once again, applying difference, similarity, contradiction, and historicity allows for a consideration of how the possibilities open to and the constraints imposed on people's working lives are neither random nor a matter of individual effort. Rather, working with experience can develop the realization that specific economic arrangements, beliefs, and social interests have to be questioned and at times transformed to enable students to increase their effective participation in determining the practices that define their working lives.

It is important to stress that exploring work experiences through either *working on* or *working with* experience should not be construed as a mere exercise in social theory. In the lesson suggestions that follow, we have tried to illustrate in the design of "units," lesson sequences that can be put in the service of expanding the range of possibilities that can be opened to people as they attempt to define their work in the world. In designing these units we do not wish to imply any necessary sequence to activities that organize *working on* and *working with* experiences. Within these pages you will find no formulae. We have written the units to illustrate how lesson ideas and the organization of such ideas into practical units can manifest a pedagogy of possibility.

NOTES

1. Our use of the concept "forms" contrasts with the conventional language of "choice," which constructs an image of free and self-evident options for living. In contrast, social forms emphasize the constituted and regulated character of possibility within everyday life.

2. See Roger I. Simon, *Teaching against the Grain*. Bergin & Garvey, in press.

3. David Snedden, "Fundamental Distinctions between Liberal and vocational education," *Curriculum Inquiry*, 7 (Spring 1977):51.

4. J. Dewey, "Education vs. Trade Training: Dr. Dewey's Reply," *Curriculum Inquiry*, 7 (Spring 1977):38.

5. See, for example, Ministry of Education, Senior Division, *Work and Employability Skills Program*. Support document to "Guidance, Senior Division," 1977; and Grady Kimbrell, and Ben S. Vineyard, *Succeeding in the World of Work* (Encino, CA: Bennett & McKnight, 1986).

6. Roger I. Simon, *Teaching Against the Grain*. Bergin & Garvey, in press.

7. Roger I. Simon, and Don Dippo, "What Schools Can Do: Designing Programs for Work Education that Challenge the Wisdom of Experience," *Journal of Education*, 169, no. 3 (1987):109.

2

Strategies for Critical Reflection in Work Education

The curriculum and teaching suggestions provided in Chapters 3–13 of this book emphasize the importance of both learning *how* to do work and learning *about* work through critical inquiry. As we have stated, our aim is to work with students in such a way as to enable them to participate more fully and effectively in determining the practices that inform their working lives. Furthermore, as we also have indicated, our pedagogical approach focuses on the central task of helping students to work both on and with their experiences to deepen their sense of how the requirements of the work world have been shaped. Such an understanding is crucial to formulating practices that might alter existing requirements and expand possibilities. For this reason, we are highly supportive of work education programs that make student work experiences central to a course of study. Such programs provide a rich opportunity for the form of critical inquiry suggested in the following chapters. However, for such an inquiry to take place, it is necessary that work-study programs provide a substantial amount of time and space for in-class discussion and analysis in relation to student work experiences. Thus reflective learning[1] must be considered central to any form of work education.

It is important to consider reflective learning as a process that moves back and forth between in-school sessions and workplace experiences. The energy for teaching and learning flows continually in both directions: to the workplace for observation and application, and from the workplace for description, clarification, judgment, and interpretation.

Neither direction is more important than the other. It is this regular and ongoing interaction that makes possible a conceptually informed practice and a practically informed understanding of work.

By using in-class time to alert students what to watch for while at work, teachers can highlight general topics, specific concepts, and skills that will enrich in-class inquiry later on in the course. In addition, students can be encouraged to bring back aspects of their workplace experience for consideration and study within the classroom. It should be clear then that reflective learning refers to more than just debriefing, more than open-ended discussions of "what's been happening at work since the last time we met to talk." It can start there, but it requires focus and form, things that the contents of this book are intended to suggest.

THE DUAL MEANING OF "STRATEGY": TECHNIQUE AND POLITICAL PRACTICE

In offering a chapter entitled "Strategies for Critical Reflection in Work Education" we do not mean to suggest that one can reduce the discussion of teaching strategies to a set of de-conceptualized tips and techniques that can be used to meet predefined, given objectives. While we of course do not diminish the importance of practical ideas and useful knowledge, we view such considerations as insufficient in and of themselves. If our version of work education is to live up to the aspirations we have set for it in our introductory chapter, we must insist that the notion of strategy also embody a particular view of what knowledge is of most worth, what it means to know something, and how we might construct representations of ourselves, others, and our shared physical and social environment. This means that strategies are about both what teachers and students might actually do together and what moral vision such strategies support.

Strategies can be both process- and content-oriented. Hence, the inclusion of a chapter such as "Health and Safety at Work" is a content strategy whereas the systematic and critical use of a technique like journal-writing exemplifies a process strategy. Thus the content chosen for this book and made manifest in suggestions for classroom practice provides the overall sense of strategy at work here. The techniques adapted to our overall framework are likely to be familiar to teachers. The question, however, is how these otherwise familiar techniques can be used in the service of a critical pedagogy of work education. Throughout we try to make clear how these techniques can be taken up as process strategies that bring into play forms of critical inquiry that arise from working on and with experience. Personal and individual reflection is expanded in each case into a collective inquiry that foregrounds contradictions, similarities, and differences that emerge from varying positions of gender, social class, age, and race within work sites. These are constituted not as ends in themselves, but rather as problematic, as starting points for discussion. Our aim via these strategies is to encourage students to: question taken-for-granted assumptions about work; comprehend workplaces as sites where identities are produced; see this production as a struggle over competing claims to truth and to correctness; and envisage ways in which the quality of their working lives can be improved.

RECOGNIZING THE STRATEGIC QUALITY OF TECHNIQUES

As we have indicated, "strategies," as used in this chapter and throughout the book, refer to more than teaching methods, lesson-planning, and resources. To work with a sense of strategy is to conceive of teaching and learning experiences as practices situated within a broader moral and political project. In this context, there is a related distinction to be made between teaching and pedagogy. The latter allows for an expanded conception of classroom practices that sees the classroom and the workplace as sites of production where identities, desires, directions for change, and even the taken-for-granted can be brought into view, challenged, affirmed, or transformed. The classroom is one site among others where the limitations and possibilities of student inquiry are given their shape.

To realize this notion of pedagogy requires the recognition of techniques as strategies. What would such a recognition require? Consider, for example, the difference between teaching students interview skills as forms of abstracted knowledge and teaching interview skills in a way that makes apparent why such capabilities are vital both to the encouragement of student inquiry generally, and to the practice of a critical pedagogy in particular. To make such a distinction would require moving beyond tips for successfully conducting interviews to communicating a sense of how interviews might contribute to the project of enabling students to begin to participate in determining the practices that inform their working lives. It is in this sense that techniques are expanded into strategies. What follows in this chapter is a more detailed discussion of specific teaching and learning strategies that can be used to encourage critical inquiry into workplace experience.

WORKING COLLECTIVELY

Working collectively constitutes a set of strategies that encourages students to move beyond individual modes of learning and problem-solving. Such strategies expand both the substance of what can be known and the range of activities through which knowledge can be acquired. From the point of view of a critical pedagogy of work education, why is working collectively important?

First of all, working collectively helps to make visible both the similarities and the differences that inform our experiences of the world. Working collectively affords us the opportunity to explore how shared experiences can often be obscured by individual understandings that leave us disconnected from each other. Conversely, in the voicing of these individual experiences we can begin to comprehend how the social realities of others influence their participation in the complexities of everyday life. This means recognizing that people are situated differently in regard to such relations as gender, class, and race, and therefore negotiate the world around them in different ways. Without the recognition of these similarities and differences, we can only arrive at limited individual solutions in our attempts to fulfill our aspirations for a better life. By working collectively, we can begin to understand the necessary common ground on which more comprehensive and effective solutions can be devised for expanding the range of possibilities open to people.

Second, working collectively is a practice of teaching and learning that brings into view questions of what we know and how we come to know what we know. It is a practice that allows us at once to validate our own experiences and knowledge while simultaneously providing an occasion to question it in order to discover alternate possibilities for interpretation. In this context, working collectively helps to mitigate the problem of the fragmentation of learning. In an effort to promote more effective and efficient knowledge acquisition, teachers have often been encouraged to employ forms of curriculum and teaching that reduce what a student needs to know to small, manageable bits of information. While this may help some students by simplifying their learning tasks, it also reduces students' ability to recognize the very real complexity and interconnectedness of social and physical settings within which we live our lives. There are, of course, always constraints on learning imposed by factors such as student abilities, time available, and the access one has to information. The point here, however, is that working collectively can be a mode in which the effect of these constraints is reduced through the sharing of learning tasks, information found, discoveries made, and insights won.

Working collectively implies a kind of pedagogy that foregrounds questions of student voice and experience. This means, by necessity, creating a classroom atmosphere that is supportive and one in which students are also encouraged to take risks. However, it should also be noted that working collectively gives important recognition to the notions of conflict and difference among our views of ourselves and our world. In other words, working collectively does not imply an extensive "happy harmony" among a group through time. Rather, it recognizes that differences will arise. Instead of suppressing and covering over such differences, working collectively acknowledges such realities as a resource for learning.

What then is needed in order to establish a classroom in which working collectively serves the interests of a critical pedagogy? Clearly, a basic sense of interpersonal trust and respect must be fostered. People must be willing to share their successes and failures and to communicate agreements and disagreements. This will also require cultivating a sense of patience as students try to engage each other. This will mean learning to respect each other's teaching and learning capacities so that students need not rely solely on the comments of the teacher. Will they consider alternative points of view? Will they accept challenges to the wisdom of their own experience? Clearly then, questions of group dynamics and communication skills are of vital concern. Thus common techniques for enhancing group work such as "name-game" introductory activities, trust exercises, or group problem-solving simulations can be turned into important strategies when seen as practices that support the purposes of working collectively discussed above.

What is essential to this process of expanding techniques of group work into strategies is the rejection of teaching communication skills in the abstract. The key here instead is always to locate these skills, both for oneself and for one's students, as aids in the wider context of developing an ability to work on and with experience. Importantly, communication skills, as well as the notions of trust and respect upon which they are grounded, are as applicable to teacher-student relations as they are to relations among students themselves. This quality of trust and respect is, of course, affected by the myriad forms of daily interaction teachers and students experience in classrooms. However, what we particularly want to stress here is that such respect and trust can in part be fostered by making the dual sense of strategy apparent for all participants in the learning process.

ENGAGING STUDENT EXPERIENCES

Students come into the classroom already knowing. The question is: How do we view what it is that they know? A critical pedagogy recognizes that our claims to knowledge are socially produced and that we each participate in different ways in that production. Given this, we are able to address the question "how could things be otherwise?" by focusing on the simultaneous interrelation between circumstances and selves. In other words, the classroom is not a site for transmission of knowledge as truth, but rather is a site for the interrogating of competing claims to truth. This is an interrogation that takes into account how such claims reference the grounds on which they are constructed. In the context of engaging student experience in the classroom this means helping students to work on their experiences to reveal their produced and contingent character. How might this be done?

What is basic to helping students *work on* their experiences is establishing a record of such experiences that is adequate for the task of beginning the process of critical reflection. One such technique for doing this is the familiar practice of student journal-writing. In order to expand this activity from technique to strategy, one must consider how journal-writing is to enter the teaching-learning process. It enters as a form of dialogic communication between teacher and students that provides an alternative to purely verbal classroom discussion. It expands the range of forms provided to students for realizing their capacities in a learning context. This is not simply a matter of providing for different "learning styles." Rather, it is the recognition that the circumstances of a serious interrogating of experience may require forms of communication that are produced in private and that require extra time for thought and response.

To clarify this further it is important to distinguish between journals and what may commonly be referred to as "logs." For example, in the workplace, logs constitute an account of the tasks a student has undertaken at the workplace in a given period of time. They are extremely useful for record-keeping. Journals, however, record the circumstances of experience *and* the observations, reactions, questions, judgments, and feelings elicited. Illustrations of issues students might choose to write about include: commenting on and attempting to clarify personal reactions to the work itself, the workplace, or the people who work there; posing questions about the work process that are being raised by other workers; narrating important incidents and tracing their effects on people; and clarifying challenges to their prospective work identities and future plans.

These then become resources for critical reflection. Such reflection can be established through in-class collective work using journals (as we illustrate in many of the subsequent units) and/or more private reflections initiated in the context of a written dialogue between teacher and student. In both cases, journals are vehicles for empowering students to insert their own stories, their own concerns and understandings into the learning process. In the context of a critical pedagogy, this also has the effect of supporting students in claiming a visible presence in relation to the structures and circumstances that shape all our lives.

While journal-writing is a practice familiar to many teachers it may be useful to briefly stress a few issues that may affect its successful use. As with activities intended to enhance students' abilities to work collectively, explaining to the class the reasons for including journal-writing in the course can be important. Journal-writing takes practice; the best time to begin is early in the course. While many of the classroom suggestions detailed in the chapters to follow indicate specific assignments that can be done with journals, students should also be encouraged to write journal entries that reflect their own questions and concerns.[2] The best way to continue and encourage the development of such writing is for the teacher to respond individually to such efforts without attention to correcting grammar and spelling. Most often this should be initiated in the spirit of confidentiality, while allowing for the possible "going public" of particular observations or questions, if the student gives permission to do so. In some cases it may be useful to engage in a collective decision as to who should have access to student journals. Who can students expect to read what they have written—the teacher, other students, guidance counselors or other school staff, or workplace supervisors? When the students themselves participate in making decisions about confidentiality, they can commit themselves more responsibly to the journal-writing process.

If work-study programs are seen solely as forms of job training, the question may arise as to whether or not students should be allowed to express judgments about work placements in their journal writing—in particular, negative judgments. In the context of a critical pedagogy of work education this question is misplaced. Judgments of any sort are forms of experience that need to be explored, questioned, and reworked in the face of competing claims to truth, and also the circumstances that have generated such claims. It should also be remembered that judgments imply questions and that this sense of questioning one's taken-for-granted realities is one of the aims of a critical pedagogy. In addition, education as a moral and political practice cannot suppress the responsibility to help students make judgments about desirable forms of social life.

The process of centering the classroom as a place where knowledge claims are explored and judgments made has profound implications well beyond the issues of journal-writing. Take, for instance, the question of defining the key concepts presented and discussed during a course—concepts such as work, skill, authority, responsibility, initiative. In many classrooms, the official textbook for the course is the authoritative source for such definitions; in other cases it is the teacher. In such contexts, the student role is to memorize definitions produced elsewhere by people other than themselves.

To accomplish critical reflection in work-study education, however, it is important to include students in the process of defining key concepts to be used during a course. For one thing, this encourages their active involvement in learning; even more importantly, it can demonstrate to them how intricately concepts, definitions, and analysis are interrelated within the process of making sense of workplace experience. What might this mean for practice? At the very least it would require helping students to question the basis on which concepts are offered as useful and important. It means seeing a text, other students, or the teacher as a source of ideas that are already in themselves responses to particular interests and concerns. It is such interests and concerns that should be made evident, if possible. In this way students can assess particular ways of seeing the world for their potential in assisting their participation in the determination of the practices that define their working lives.

LEARNING FROM OTHERS

As parents and teachers we sometimes despair when youth reject the offer of our wisdom and experience. But such rejection should come as no surprise; learning from the experiences of others is not something easily done. In work-study programs not only is learning to be accomplished through texts that report on the experiences of others, but as well, students are expected to make good use of the opportunity to observe and talk with experienced people in the workplace. Often the systematic practice of observation and interviewing skills is introduced into such programs in order to enhance the possibilities for learning in these situations. Indeed, observing and interviewing in the workplace are incorporated into many of the lesson suggestions in the following units. However, the question at this moment is: How does one expand observing and interviewing from a set of techniques for collecting information to part of the strategies that form a critical pedagogy of work education?

We want to return for a moment to the distinction between working with and working on experience in the previous chapter. Recall that we said that this distinction had to be understood in connection with the basic task of setting the categories of difference, similarity, contradiction, and historicity into relation with our daily activities and commonsense understandings. In other words, questions were to be posed regarding similarities and differences among and within different versions of practice and common sense; contradictions in this regard were to be identified and questioned, and the origins of what we take for granted were to be explored and made problematic. While such ideas may seem at first glance complex and disconnected from the all-too-real issues of classroom practice, in our view they provide the framework that is necessary in order to move from technique to strategy when asking students to engage in activities like interviewing and observing.

Consider this example drawn from an interview with three students:

A male high school student is completing part of his school program by working in an upholstery shop. He has a desire to be an upholsterer; he likes working with his hands and completing upholstery projects in school and at home has given him a sense of satisfaction. In the shop he meets another worker who tells him: "You're crazy 'cause upholstery is going right out." He says to the student, "I hate upholstery and I never forgave my dad for putting me in it. I think you're crazy to go into upholstery." The student then confronted the worker with the question: "So why are you still working in an upholstery shop?" The worker replies, "That's all I can do." In discussion of this incident, the students suggest that the worker ought to go shovel garbage if he thinks the work is so bad; he (the worker) shouldn't go around "putting down" other people's desires.

In this example, the student defensively dismisses what the worker had to say about his experience of working because it contradicted his own future work identity. Why? The student had developed his affinity for upholstery work in the school shop. School shops like upholstering and woodworking are commonly organized around individual projects in which skills development and a sense of craft and quality are stressed. It was little wonder then that the student's first experience of industrial upholstery work led to a contradiction in what he understood upholstering is and should be. So strong was the student's ideal that he could not see or hear the "bad news" embodied in the pain and disillusionment of an experienced worker. Yet this too is part of the reality this student was confronted with on the job. Acknowledging this means that a critical pedagogy of work education requires more than an observation or interview that simply documents (and then dismisses) such realities. It must include a process of listening and coming to grips with how it is that the experience of others at work comes to be so different from our own and of what relevance such an understanding would have for our future working lives.

The question is: What kind of interviewing skills and mode of understanding of other people's talk about their work would encourage a consideration of such learning opportunities beyond their ability to confirm one's current understanding? At the very least, such skills and analysis must enable students to consider how the possibilities open to, and the constraints imposed upon, people's working lives are not random or a matter of individual effort. In other words, the key to moving beyond the systematic documentation of what other people do or say is to find ways of understanding how their views have been informed by factors that have organized and regulated their experiences. This, of course, is too abstract a statement to be easily put into practice. Suggestions as to how such efforts can be made concrete and put in the context of questions of interest to students will be given in the lesson suggestions to come.

CONTEXTUALIZING THE CURRICULUM

For many students the experience of school is one of a seemingly arbitrary flow of texts, activities, and assignments. They are most often positioned passively in relation to the aims and questions that motivate the curriculum to which they are exposed. Yet we know that students can only be engaged in a serious exploration of something as complex as work and work experience if they are able to form their own sense of interest and need to understand. But how does this happen?

Of course, in any form of work-study education we expect such interests and questions to be generated from the experiences of students and those of other workers in the workplace. Additionally, given the opportunity for in-school critical reflection, the continual interplay between work site and school might be expected to deepen such generation of interests and questions. However, at this point we wish to stress another source of interest and questions—the initial form and substance of a course of study provided by the teacher. We wish to recognize that teachers have a clear responsibility to help students confront new information that might produce insights and questions that they had never thought of before. The issue here is how this might be done in a way consistent with a critical pedagogy of work education.

Part of the responsibility of a critical pedagogy is to make visible its own production in terms of both the content and process strategies that it uses. This means that a teacher following this approach would always be careful to try to clearly explain and contextualize why a given unit is being studied and how particular activities are consistent with the purposes of such a unit. Why is this so important? By doing this it allows students to see the questions and issues that have motivated the curricula that is giving structure to learning. This is important because it allows students as well as teachers to understand how classroom activities might be recognized as strategies consistent with the pursuit of a moral and political vision. In other words, students as well as teachers must recognize the dual sense of strategy referred to at the beginning of this chapter. This means students should not only be engaged in the details of classroom techniques but also in judging and challenging the relation between such techniques and the social visions they support.

In the chapters that follow, you will find a set of introductory comments that provide a rationale for the content and activities also specified. One of the ways in which teachers and students can generate a shared sense of purpose for any given lesson suggestion or learning activity is through discussion of some of the ideas put forward in these introductory sections. The sections have not been written as texts to be distributed to students (although in some cases teachers may choose to do so), but rather as frames of reference from which teachers can draw when introducing new topics and activities to their class. In addition, teachers may also choose to contextualize the existence of work-study programs in their schools. For example, cooperative education is so new in many school board jurisdictions that its own history, including the issues and controversies surrounding it (see, for example, chapter 3), may be usefully discussed with a class. By doing so, students can more clearly see, question, and challenge their own location within the work-study process, raising questions themselves as to how work education should be conceived.

NOTES

1. The term "reflective learning" is used here to directly acknowledge the terminology now existent in Ontario which mandates the examination of work and work experience in the context of existing work-study programs. Guidelines for using cooperative education in Ontario schools require the provision of class time for "reflective learning." The inclusion of this curricula agenda was won as part of an effort to prevent the collapse of such programs into an exclusively skills-training emphasis. In the context of this book, "reflective learning" refers to a specific form of inquiry informed by the framework of critical pedagogy.

2. It should be recognized that journals might include photographs, poetry, diagrams, and drawings as ways of enhancing the expression of student experience. However, it will be important to remember that the mode of expression will influence the facility for using journal-writing in the context of critical reflection.

II

Exploring Technical Relations

3

Working Knowledge: What It Takes to Do the Job

What do we mean when we say that someone is a "competent" participant in a workplace? What does it mean to say that someone has a good working knowledge of how things are done? These are complex questions. Knowing what to do and how to do it often requires much more than technical training. Knowing your job often means understanding how work requirements are shaped by the particular organizations in which those requirements take place. An education that helps students understand their current work realities so as to be able to transform them requires a consideration of this relationship. In this chapter we approach this through the concept of "working knowledge."

Working knowledge includes more than just the notion of a technical ability to perform certain tasks such as typing invoices, back-stitching upholstery, using micrometers, supervising outdoor play, washing hair, making cheesecake, developing photographs. These are of course included in the meaning of the concept, but there is much more. Each and every task in a workplace is embedded in a particular set of social relations within which people define the facts, skills, procedures, values, and beliefs relevant to particular jobs in their own organizations. For this reason job competency often means understanding how the particularities of one's workplace define what one needs to know to get a job done. Perhaps more to the point, there is no work in the abstract; there is only work in context. "Learning work" thus often entails not only the development of technical and social skills but also an ability to understand how and why such skills are used, modified, and supplemented in different situations.

It is the premise of this chapter that the notion of "working knowledge" is a useful concept for the study of how people in different workplaces define what is important to know in order to be competent workers and do competent work. However, to employ working knowledge as a conceptual tool in such study requires that we be more specific about the particular aspects of working life referred to by this concept.

The following is a partial list of different workplace features that suggests some things it might be important to know in order to be an effective worker in any given workplace. This list will be helpful to students as they begin to describe and question what working knowledges seem to be required at their workplaces. This is not an exhaustive list. Rather, it is intended to facilitate the analysis of work experience through a consideration of a variety of knowledges required in various situations.

Workplace materials—material objects that are basic to a workplace. These include for example: tools, equipment, decor, supplies, raw materials, and finished products, clothing.

The language of work—the specialized words and phrases, technical jargon, abbreviations, codes and forms as well as names, nicknames, slang, cliches, tones of voice, gestures, and modes of conversation.

Workplace "facts"—the information and beliefs taken as objectively true, incontrovertible, and accurate by at least some group of people in a workplace. These "facts" include not only task-related information but also reputations, workplace customs, rituals, and traditions.

Skills and techniques—the set of capacities and competencies necessary to perform certain procedures and complete certain tasks required by the organization of work in a particular workplace.

The frame of reference for evaluating workplace events—the principles used by workers to determine the good or bad qualities of things, people, events, and/or ideas; for example, the criteria used by others to determine a "fair day's work," a "job well done," a "good supervisor," or a "harebrained scheme."

Rules and meanings—the implicit and explicit rules, understandings and expectations that regulate interactions among people in various situations. Implicated in these are power structures, lines and areas of authority, questions of responsibility, status, prestige, and influence.

It is crucial to emphasize that these forms of working knowledge are always situationally organized. As such their manifestations in each workplace will reflect a variety of forms of influence ranging from market forces, capital available for technological expenditures, existing forms of division of labor, the gendered character of work in a given workplace, and so on. This is another way of saying that there is not simply one coherent working knowledge for a particular type of work or occupation. Working knowledge cannot be understood in abstract, general terms. It is found in particular workplaces, produced and regulated by a complex range of determinations.

In our view it is important to emphasize the complexity and origins of the particular situated character of specific forms of working knowledge. This importance is not arbitrary. The perspective on work education taken in this book suggests that not only is it desirable to understand what is required to be considered a competent worker; but as well it is fundamental that students understand the bases, consequences, and alternatives to such requirements. This position would include an understanding of:

- how it happens that different people have differential access to various forms of working knowledge
- why it is that differential access to various forms of working knowledges results in different consequences in terms of for example: status, pay, employment opportunity, and health
- why differences in what is required to be a competent worker exist among workplaces
- what possible alternatives might exist for defining what it means to be a competent worker

This chapter is organized in the following sections:

- Theme I: Introducing the notion of "working knowledge"—Activities One and Two
- Theme II: Becoming an insider: Gaining access to and developing working knowledge—Activities Three and Four
- Theme III: Values applied to working knowledge: Grasping the sense in which working knowledge is not neutral—Activity Five
- Theme IV: Celebrating and acknowledging "becoming competent"—Activity Six

The general concept of working knowledge may provide an interesting and useful focus or theme for work-study courses—one that, once introduced, can be returned to again and again. Teaching and learning about working knowledge in the in-school component will involve the consideration of very real, very concrete everyday experiences on the job.

All students, therefore, should be able to handle and benefit from the topics, assignments, discussions, and exercises used to achieve this chapter's objectives. Of course, their abilities to analyze the working knowledge of their workplaces is something that will develop over time; that is why the suggestion is made that the chapter not be treated in a time-bound way. Rather than looking at working knowledge once, we suggest that it is a topic worth coming back to several times during the length of the course. Indeed, the four themes of this chapter have been written in a way appropriate to the continual interrogating of working knowledge during the entire period of a student's work placement; that is, the activities in each theme can be used at different points in time in the course sequence.

Teaching Note

The premise of the activities of this chapter (as it is of this book) is that learning is not simply a process of acquisition but rather one of production. That is, one's knowledge is produced through the activities of observation, questioning, discussion, writing, debate, and exchange. This is the significance of our notion of work-study pedagogy: that it will assist students to make sense of work and working. Rather than "receiving" working knowledge, students (individually and together) will be producing their grasp of working knowledge by identifying it, interrogating it, assessing it, understanding its basis, and determining the consequences of it for their future working lives.

Within this pedagogical process teachers will often have to develop strategies for responding to differences of opinion expressed in the class. People will have a variety of background experiences, and thus a variety of resources for making sense out of work and working. Co-op workplaces themselves will differ in the working knowledges they produce and use. For these reasons, in the normal course of events in co-op, a wide variety of knowledge claims will be presented about work and working, from an equally wide variety of sources.

As in any form of teaching that emphasizes group discussion, the question arises as to how to treat the status of individual knowledge claims regarding the topic at hand. In our view, it is important that the matter of handling differences of opinion be dealt with explicitly at the beginning of a course. While any pedagogy that often proceeds from student experiences must of course support and encourage a range of student voices in the classroom, the question remains as to how the class should encourage and respond to the variety of forms through which students express themselves. Should all statements have the same status? What level of evidence is a student responsible for presenting when making a knowledge claim? Can one differentiate opinions from knowledge claims? Is it possible to separate fact from value? How should overtly racist or sexist statements be responded to? What should be the place of a teacher's knowledge and expertise in such discussions?

THEME I: INTRODUCING THE NOTION OF WORKING KNOWLEDGE

The purpose of the activities in Theme I is to introduce students to the notion of working knowledge and provide them with an opportunity to begin using this concept as a way of questioning and comprehending the nature of work in their work placements. The basic approach taken by these activities uses the previously given list of different types of knowledges in order to examine aspects of working knowledge required in different situations.

Activity One

Viewing films about work is a simple and concrete way of introducing the concept of working knowledge to a class. Many short (15–20 minute) films that portray particular forms of work are available for classroom use. The National Film Board of Canada (NFB) is a particularly good resource for such films. If time allows it would be desirable to use two or three films which contrast different types of work. For example, the film *Wilf* (NFB, 1968) about subsistence farming would contrast sharply with *Something of Value* (NFB, 1977), which details the work of homemaking.

In developing this activity it is suggested that teachers review a number of short films that depict different types of work prior to their use in class. Films should be used that portray some aspect of all six categories of working knowledge listed in the introductory section of this chapter.

What to Do in the Classroom

Introduce the concept of working knowledge as that which a person needs to know in order to be considered a knowledgeable or competent worker. Distribute and discuss descriptions of the six categories with students. Ask for additional examples or suggestions of new categories.

As students watch the film have them list examples of the six (or more) types of working knowledges depicted in the film.

Using the board or chart paper, list and discuss the various features of working knowledge observed by the class for each of the categories. It should be emphasized that a clear understanding of different types of working knowledges will be necessary in order to complete the next activity.

Teaching Note

Before beginning Activity One it would be useful to explain to the class that this activity is in itself a preparatory exercise that will help students with more complex assignments that will focus on the work taking place at their own work placements (see, for example, Activity Two). Activity One is a rather straight-forward guided analysis of the working knowledge depicted in films. In our experience some students may find this exercise somewhat boring and pointless— especially when asked to analyze forms of work they have little interest or in-vestment in. Part of the challenge to the teacher is to attempt to help students situate any specific classroom activity or student assignment within a larger set of questions and learning objectives. When students experience a course as a series of unconnected and seemingly arbitrary assignments imposed by the teacher, the opportunity for student learning is diminished. Thus in this case, we suggest that the teacher introduce the purposes of Theme I and a plan of activities for accomplishing those purposes prior to beginning any specific activity.

Activity Two

Photography as tool for learning is well suited to the objectives of having students reflect upon their work experiences. Photography in-volves thinking about a situation, and about what one is trying to capture on film and what would be the best way to do it. The choice of what to photograph embodies the frame of reference through which students make sense of their own experiences. Thus the use of photographs for discussion and analysis can be quite effective in helping students to interrogate the adequacy of their grasp of the working knowledges re-quired by their work placements.

The basic objective of this activity is to have students interrogate the working knowledges required in their own workplaces through the pro-cess of re-presenting aspects of these knowledges through the medium of photography. Where a teacher deems it appropriate and practical, videos might be used for similar purposes. What is important to com-prehend here is the significance of employing a visual medium as a vehicle for articulating and presenting student understanding of working knowledge. Quite often aspects of working knowledge are tacit and difficult to express in words alone. In helping students articulate what they understand to be the working knowledges of their workplace, visual representations like photographs can provide an alternative form of expression and a concrete point of reference for discussion. Understood as deliberate "ways of seeing," photographs also allow for a consider-ation of what is missing from such representations and why this is so.

Teaching Note

If a teacher has not used photography in the classroom before there are a few things that might be considered. It is useful to familiarize students with the operation of the camera they will be using. A fully automatic 35mm camera is probably best but Polaroid and Instamatic cameras will suffice. Cameras are not needed for every student in class. Most students will be able to take the required number of photographs in a day. Therefore, set up a procedure whereby students can get cameras to each other. If students see each other frequently, this isn't much of a problem. If, as sometimes is the case in co-operative education programs, students are out of touch with each other when they are on the job, a pick-up and delivery system will have to be established.

What to Do in the Classroom.

After securing the permission of their employers, students are assigned to take one role of 24 pictures at their workplace. Ask students to take a number of pictures that capture certain elements of working knowledge. For example, four pictures of aspects of workplace material (tools, clothes), four pictures that illustrate particular or unique forms of language use at one's workplace, and four pictures that illustrate important workplace "facts."

Once the photographs have been developed they can then be used as the basis for individual or group assignments within which students can further improve their capability to employ the concept of working knowledge. For example, individual students can be given an assignment to construct an illustrated presentation (through captioning or montage) using the photographs they have taken in order "to introduce a new worker to your workplace." Within groups, students working in similar placements might collaborate to produce a presentation attempting to illustrate what it would be like to work in a particular occupation.

While the purpose at this introductory stage of the chapter is to help students develop a basic understanding of the concept of working knowledge, class discussion and/or evaluation of student assignments will usually provide the opportunity for teachers and students to raise some of the more complex questions about the various determinations of forms of working knowledge. Such questions might include:

• Why do differences exist in the working knowledges required by different organizations that produce similar goods and services?

• What range of knowledges seem to make a person into a "specialized" worker? Is work organized so that it is easy or difficult for other people to acquire such knowledge if they so wish? Are there any special consequences that people experience as a result of being "specialized"?

• Do women and men seem to have access to the same range of working knowledges in the workplace? If not, what do you think are the reasons for this?

Teaching Note

If such questions are not raised by students (although quite often they are raised, both by students who do and do not have strong records of academic achievement!) It is the teacher's responsibility to raise them. That is, it is the teacher's responsibility to direct discussion toward an increasingly complex understanding of how work and work requirements are constituted in our society. This responsibility follows from our belief that such an understanding is possible for most students and desirable in that it will help them comprehend what it would take to expand the range of possibilities they will have for living and working.

THEME II: BECOMING AN INSIDER: GAINING ACCESS TO AND DEVELOPING WORKING KNOWLEDGE

Learning how one can gain access to working knowledge is important to one's ability to move from being an outsider in the workplace to becoming an insider—that is, one who is knowledgeable in the ways that things are done there. If students can increase their sensitivity to the ways this process is accomplished and the ways they can enhance their own ability to participate in this process, they will develop a way of "learning work" which they will be able to reuse and refine several times during their work lives. The following are three alternative suggestions for helping students focus on how working knowledge is acquired.

Activity Three

The following are several options that can be initiated either in the context of a regular process of journal-writing or within specific assignments.

What to Do in the Classroom

> When I think about all the stupid things we've done to the new trainees!... Like, when Tom first started, we sent him down to look for a can of steam for the Danish... and he's down there looking around for a can of steam and he comes back up and says, "I can't find it," right?... And then we got him to go down and get some glue to glue the sesame seeds on the bun. And he flies down looking for glue, right?... And, uh, there was another new person that started and we got him to count stir sticks.... He had them in, you know, six rows of 10... and we were all just killing ourselves laughing.
>
> (Liz at a fast food place)

Have students document the variety of ways they were welcomed or introduced to the organization within which they are working. Encourage students to describe anything that happened that they would identify as a welcoming or introduction procedure. This might range from formal interviews with employers to being taken out to lunch by a fellow worker. It might also, as one student recalls above, include some slightly embarrassing experiences like jokes, tricks, and other forms of ritual initiation. Ask students to try to distinguish between types of knowledge they were explicitly told about by employers and employees and types that were left for students to figure out on their own.

Teaching Note

Sometimes students will tell "crazy" stories that provoke laughter. Moments like these, while helping to build a sense of conviviality in the class, can also, on occasion, be ambiguous. Teachers can find themselves having to decide whether to open up a particular story for discussion, or to let it pass simply as an enjoyable moment. Consider, for example, this brief excerpt from one of David's stories about his first few days at a machine shop:

The other guys, they were always jokin' around. . . . There was this new guy, eh? And he was totally confused. One of the guys, Mark, he showed him some nude pictures, and Mark goes, "Yeah, this is my wife and she really was fat," eh. And the new guy, he believed it, right? . . . And the rest of them, they really started laughing. A lot of times they joke around like that.

Experiences like these, while clearly an instance of "initiation" into workplace relations, are nevertheless also important for the often taken-for-granted ways of thinking they reproduce. Showing explicit pictures, in this case, may be a good joke, but at whose expense and at what cost? What is important about humor is that it is always contextualized—what relations of gender are reproduced in this moment at the shop? And later, when it's retold in class?

While we all make mistakes in new situations, it is not always that easy to learn from our mistakes. Different people "learn" different things from the same mistakes. Ask students to discuss mistakes they have made so far, what seemed to result from these mistakes, what they have concluded as a result, and why. Ask students to consider whether and under what circumstances "learning from mistakes" might be an effective way to develop working knowledge.

Teaching Note

Some students may be reluctant to talk about situations in which they ended up feeling uncomfortable or foolish. While a supportive learning environment within which people share some of their embarrassments and focus on them as opportunities for learning (and not simply a voyeuristic occasion for a laugh) can help alleviate this feeling, students should not be forced into a public confession which they feel simply displays their incompetence. This will be particularly important for students who do not need their previous inability to meet someone else's requirements emphasized yet again.

Have students identify additional information that would help them perform their jobs more effectively. Then have them consider the possible ways such information might be obtained. Answers may range from asking the boss, to looking for an instruction or operating manual, asking co-workers, or experimenting on one's own. Compare the ease with which different students feel they would be able to obtain such information. Are there features of the workplace that encourage the seeking of new knowledge? Are there other features that encourage covering up one's lack of knowledge? In light of these questions, have students consider what would have to be done to enable them to have more access to this kind of working knowledge.

Teaching Note

It is important to develop a sense of how to structure the discussion that will ensue as a result of initiating any of the above alternative activities. It is our suggestion that teachers emphasize, in their own contributions, observations about the way students are learning the working knowledges of their workplaces. It is important that students grasp the complexity of this process and the fact that effective learning is influenced not only by individual differences in previous knowledge and self-confidence but also factors such as the structural distribution of information in the workplace and the particular terms of reference of their co-op assignments that limit what students, employees, and employers think it is legitimate for co-op students to do or ask. Understanding this complexity is part of learning to be able to develop a capability to define one's work in the world.

Activity Four

A familiarity with everyday workplace language is often considered basic to being competent or knowledgeable in one's workplace. Here is a simple classroom game that will help students focus on the language particularities of their workplace and the way in which they gained access to these particularities.

What to Do in the Classroom

The following is a game that can be played either between teams of students or with students as individual competitors. After students have been at their workplaces for a short while, have them think of a word or term or phrase (i.e., any specialized bit of language) that was unfamiliar to them when they first began at their workplace and that they think no one else in the class will be able to define; "define" in this sense means to identify the meaning that the word has at the student's workplace. Some of the words, terms, or phrases that students have previously used during this game are:

- "circle" (from daycare centers). Note: different centers define this word differently.
- "mike" (from machine shops). Spelling is an issue here, because the word is "micrometer" and the spelling might be considered to be "mic."
- "runout" and "bar stock." Both are machinist terms.
- "IC's"—little red lights that you put on printed circuit boards.
- "perm rod"—from hairdressing.
- "microfiche"—medium of reduced size storage and retrieval of large amounts of information.

If anyone can provide the correct definition, then the student (or his or her team) loses that round; if the other team or the rest of the class is indeed stumped, then the student (or his/her team) wins that round. When the game is being played, it is important that the rest of the class know the kind of workplace that the student giving the word is working at; otherwise it is far too easy to stump the rest of the class.

After the game is completed, through individual written assignment or group discussion, focus can be given to the various ways different students came to acquire an understanding of these previously unfamiliar terms. To structure this somewhat it is suggested students consider:

1. The situation within which they first gained access to this new item of working knowledge: for example, who used the term? Was it in written or spoken language? When did they use it? What were they doing and/or to whom were they speaking? What were they talking about when the term or phrase was used? Was it the word, term, or phrase that was new and strange or was it a familiar word with a new and strange meaning? Was the contextual referent for the expression the relationship, organization, occupation, or something else?

2. The initial consequences of the students' lack of familiarity: for example, how did it come about that the student was in a position to hear or see this term used? How did not understanding the term make the student feel? Did the lack of familiarity with the term or phrase affect the student's ability to do his or her job?

3. The way the student became familiar with this item of working knowledge:

for example, if the student did not understand the meaning of the particular term, what did he or she do about it?

Teaching Note

Some students may see nothing at all problematic in the way they acquired the new term; for others, however, gaining access to the new knowledge may have been a bit more difficult, requiring some initiative and courage to get an explanation. Students may also downplay the importance of their job assignment and physical location within the workplace work processes in influencing their opportunities to get access to new knowledge. It is important for the teacher to focus the assignment or discussion on the reality that access to new working knowledge is not necessarily straightforward and is not just a matter of individual initiative and responsibility but is also influenced by the status and structural location of a worker. Indeed, an understanding of this fact can raise important questions about how the work organization prevents workers from having a comprehensive understanding of the working knowledges used within a workplace and how this process is used to control items like status, wages, or opportunities for promotion.

THEME III: VALUES APPLIED TO WORKING KNOWLEDGE: GRASPING THE SENSE IN WHICH WORKING KNOWLEDGE IS NOT NEUTRAL

Consider a discussion held in a co-op class after students had spent one week at their workplaces. One student, working on the security staff of a local department store, described what he had learned of the store's working knowledge about how to deal with young children caught stealing candy bars: "Scare them and make them cry—then they won't do it again." Two other students, working in different daycare centers, described their workplaces' working knowledge about how to discipline the children when they did something wrong: "Never hit them, don't scare them, always speak warmly and kindly to them."

It is clear that these vastly different working knowledges are legitimated by very different frames of reference for evaluating appropriate ways to handle the problem of deviancy in young children. That is, particular versions of working knowledge are always defined within a frame of reference of beliefs and values that give value to particular ways of doing things. This is the sense in which we mean that working knowledge is not neutral. To develop a sense of why things are the way they are, what values they support, and what would have to be done for things to be otherwise, it is necessary that students begin to understand the beliefs and values that structure the working knowledges of the variety of work organizations that can be found in our society.

Teaching Note

The basic method that we suggest for helping to raise the issue of non-neutrality of working knowledge is a process of strong contrast. That is, the teacher should try to present examples of alternative ways of doing and acting that provoke the question of how different beliefs and values are implicated in the way organizations define what it means to do competent work.

Activity Five

Since working knowledge is never found out of context, it can never be fully understood or assessed out of context. One major aspect of the context of work in contemporary Canadian society is the free-enterprise system—that is, privately owned enterprise. As an example of the extent to which we take for granted this particular context, notice how often we refer to workplaces purely and simply as "business and industry," or sometimes just "business"—even though many educative placements are in publicly funded services and agencies.

This activity utilizes the existence of worker co-operatives as an alternative mode of organizing work that embodies some versions of working knowledge that are at variance with what would be seen as desired competencies in a capitalist-owned enterprise. Lessons on worker co-ops can be given specific relevance and impact if one or more students in the class are actually placed in particular co-ops in the local community. Even without such first-hand experiences, however, students can derive considerable benefit from attention to workers' co-ops as a context within which work is organized and working knowledge is produced and utilized.

What to Do in the Classroom

Using the brief statement provided below ("What is a Worker Co-operative?") introduce the notion of worker cooperatives to the class. If possible, give examples of enterprises in your community that are co-operatively organized or ask students to investigate and find out which ones are.

Have students read "Enough is Enough!," a short case description of several problems a group of workers are having at a particular workplace (see below).

In relation to this case, identify the worker knowledge that is being undervalued by Mr. Coulter, the owner of the Chester Food Market and the person who has determined the way work in the Food Market is to be done.

Discuss how what counts as working knowledge might change if control over decision-making in the workplace were to be shared equally

among the workers. Ask the class to consider what add:tional competencies might be required under such a form of decision-making. (Note:
stress here that cooperation skills are often a "hidden" form of working
knowledge and something too often taken for granted.)

Teaching Note

*"What is a Worker Cooperative?" and "Enough is Enough!" have been
adapted from the curriculum unit* Co-operative Entrepreneurship, *published
by the Canadian Co-operative Association. This organization publishes a wide
range of material of interest to teachers of work education. Classroom ideas for
developing cooperation skills and detailed suggestions for introducing information about economic cooperatives into class discussion are available from the
association. Much of this material will be of value to teachers not only in Canada
but in other countries as well. For more information, write to: Canadian Cooperative Association, 400–275 Bank St., Ottawa, Ontario, K2L 2P4.*

What is a Worker Cooperative?

Work is a fact of life. Most of us think of work as having a job in
which we get paid for doing something for an employer. Many people
dream of being their own boss—of either working alone or having others
work for them. Another form of work, which is attracting people around
the world, is the worker cooperative.

A worker cooperative is a business owned and operated by its workers.
It is organized on the democratic principle of one vote for each worker-
owner, regardless of the amount of money he or she invests in the
business. In a worker cooperative, only those who work in the business
have a vote. Outsiders can invest in the business, but do not have a
vote. A worker cooperative can be an exciting place to work. Generally,
people enjoy their work when they are with people they like and, most
importantly, when they have some control over decision-making. The
democratic structure of a worker cooperative can provide such an
opportunity.

The democratic principle of cooperative work is exercised through
meetings. The frequency of meetings varies among cooperatives, but
many hold their general meetings once a week, every two weeks, or
once a month. At meetings, worker-owners bring up a variety of issues
ranging from "who takes out the garbage" to "how the annual surplus
(profit) will be distributed." Members can suggest ideas for new products
or services and new ways to organize work. Complaints are aired.

An issue such as what to do with the year-end surplus can generate
many opinions. Some members might suggest splitting the surplus
equally among the members, some may want to give it to a cause such

as the environmental movement, others may want to buy new equipment for the business, and still others may want to start a company dental plan. Deciding what to do with the surplus can require lengthy discussion and the final solution might be to use the money for more than one purpose. The important point is that all members are encouraged to voice their opinions freely. The final decision is usually made by a vote.

The members of a worker cooperative will have varying degrees of enthusiasm, experience, knowledge, and skill. It is an opportunity for members to contribute to each other's growth and attainment of new skills. The workers learn to work cooperatively and to exercise their right to participate in decisions affecting their workplace. The challenge is to create a business that is democratically controlled and meets the needs of the worker-owners.

Worker cooperatives are just one form of democratic economic organization. Other forms with which you may be familiar include consumer, housing, and agricultural marketing cooperatives. Many regions also have credit unions that are cooperatively owned.

Enough is Enough!

"We'll never let that happen again!" With that vow, five young workers at the Chester Food Market quit, determined to start their own business.

Andrew, Rosetta, Matt, Carol-Ann, and Jose had worked at the Chester Food Market, a small food store with a lunch counter. All of them were interested in preparing and selling food, and they had enjoyed working together. There was not really one thing that led to their mass resignation; there were just a lot of little things. More and more, they seemed to have disagreements with their boss over how they did their work and how the store was run.

"Remember the time Matt and I switched shifts and Mr. Coulter had a fit?" Rosetta laughed. "There I was trying to find a new daycare for my three-year-old in the middle of winter, juggling my shifts so I'd be at work on time, and Mr. Coulter tells me I'm 'irresponsible.' "

"He said something like that to me once. That I was . . . oh, I know," a slow smile came across Matt's face. "He said I wasted too much time talking to the customers."

"Well, he was right about some things," snapped Andrew. "You used to drive me nuts the way you chatted it up with all those people."

"Hey, it was good customer relations. I mean, I knew all the products that they wanted. And they always came back, didn't they?" Matt looked around for support.

Everyone nodded. The customers had liked Matt, and he did have some good suggestions for new products. He had thought of Mexican food long before the other stores started carrying it and making a fortune in sales. But his suggestions, like everyone else's, usually fell on deaf ears. Carol-Ann and Jose had wanted to rearrange the check-out area, so it would not be congested at busy times. But Mr. Coulter said the renovations would be too expensive. He just made a joke about them working too slowly.

Carol-Ann thought the new check-out arrangement would eventually improve business and increase profits, but so what? She would not get any of the money anyway. Jose sighed and said, "It's his store and it's his money." Carol-Ann felt sullen, and resigned herself to just doing her job and nothing more.

Three weeks later, Mr. Coulter refused to let the employees choose their own vacation days. This was the straw that "broke the camel's back" and they quit.

They had heard something about a worker co-operative in which the workers owned and organized the business. Maybe this was the ticket for them.

THEME IV: CELEBRATING AND ACKNOWLEDGING "BECOMING COMPETENT"

One of the aims of an experientially based work education is to place students in situations with which they can experience the satisfaction of meeting the challenges offered within workplace learning. Indeed, recognizing the acquisition of working knowledge as a significant accomplishment is consistent with our overall aim of helping students to clarify their potential for agency in their work lives. By focusing on what students have and can accomplish and what possibilities might be open to them if some of the ways working knowledge is constituted were changed, we can encourage a sense of possibility that will be more than simply naive hope.

Activity Six

The following are several options for activities that focus on student initiative, creativity, and accomplishment. The key in utilizing these activities is to support and encourage students in taking an active role in defining and producing a sense of being a competent worker. What is important to stress here is not only that some students may have had some remarkable experiences of agency in their workplaces, but also that students have been thoughtful and imaginative in grasping how work may have been done even if they have not had the opportunity to try out their ideas.

What to Do in the Classroom

Ask students to identify a particular problem they were experiencing at their workplace. Describe the details of the problem. What did they do (including nothing) to deal with this problem? Where did the idea for this kind of solution come from? What were the effects of the solution they chose to implement on them personally, on fellow workers, and on the workplace as a whole?

Have the students identify a specific facet of their workplace experience in which they can see that a change in how things were done would be an improvement for their own work, for their fellow workers' work, or for the workplace as a whole. What makes them think that such a change would in fact be an improvement? What would be the best way to implement this particular change? If possible, have students devise a strategy for making the change and then implement the chosen strategy. Ask them to report on what happened. What was the reaction of their supervisor and fellow workers?

Ask students to identify aspects of their own "performance" at the workplace about which they feel the greatest pride of accomplishment. Then, have them describe the history of this development of competence: What are the ingredient skills or qualities and where did they come from (including from outside the workplace)? What were the key learning experiences? At what point(s) did they begin to become aware of their own competence? What are other people's reactions to this aspect of competence, including fellow workers, employer/supervisors, and teachers?

4

Skills and Work Design

This chapter has been written as a response to the deceptively simple question: What is a skill? Ask most people to define the word "skill" and they will tell you that it refers to a person's special ability or proficiency to produce or accomplish something. In our view, this answer is inadequate and indeed dangerous. The danger is that in designating "skill" as a property of person, an ability that someone possesses, something is suppressed or forgotten which is central to helping people understand how work environments affect the capabilities of workers. What is forgotten is the notion that a skill is a practice dependent on the combination of a human capacity and the requirements and opportunities provided within a work environment. As a consequence of this idea, we think it important to emphasize that the skills people "possess" are always dependent for their development, display, and maintenance on opportunities to put them into practice. This perspective is quite different from the simple definition given above. A key aspect of this difference is that by emphasizing that skills are dependent on a combination of human capacities and job requirements and opportunities, we can sensibly pose questions such as: Is it fair to judge people's capabilities on the basis of what they are demonstrably able to do? How can a person be "de-skilled" or "re-skilled?" What sense can I make of lists that specify the skills required by a specific occupation?

Given this point of view concerning the features necessary for any adequate study of what is meant by "skills" and how one might acquire them, it is obvious that more than just individual capacities must be stressed. Capabilities and attitudes are not fixed individual traits and being acknowledged as competent is as much a social event as it is an individual one (see Chapter 3, Working Knowledge). But there is more at stake here than questions of personal capabilities. How one understands the complex processes of skill development is crucial for determining what course of action one should take when a person's actions or attitudes are deemed inadequate, inappropriate, or insufficient.

It is becoming increasingly common to hear employers complaining about low worker productivity stemming from problems such as absenteeism, turnover, strikes, sabotage, and a general reluctance by workers to commit themselves to tasks.[1] The typical comment is that workers are lazy, trying to do as little as possible. The flip side of this view is the research that shows large numbers of workers are dissatisfied with their work.

While employers and workers blame each other, everyone seems to agree that our society has now entered a "crisis in productivity and commitment." This situation has recently been seen by many government officials, business leaders, and union representatives as a fundamental threat to Canada's future, given the "new reality of global markets and stiff international economic competition." Many people are now anxiously asking: What is to be done? This is now and will continue to be a question facing all Canadians.

Solutions offered to complex problems always depend on starting assumptions and ways of seeing the issues at hand. In our view, how one is able to think about the crisis in productivity and commitment is intimately connected to how one understands the concept of skills and skill development. As an illustration, consider the different suggestions that have been made as to the origin of the problem. Simplifying matters somewhat, it is possible to see a dichotomous pattern emerging. On the one hand, there are those who claim the problem lies with workers' lack of appropriate skills. This view sees workers today (especially young workers) as lazy, expecting too much, spoiled and overprotected by government and unions, and without the moral decency of a proper work ethic. Those who hold this view advocate solutions such as calling on schools to promote a stronger sense of worker responsibility, commitment, and respect.

On the other hand, there are those who claim the productivity crisis lies in the way work is designed and defined. The point is often made that while work designs may at first glance seem efficient, they can have negative effects on workers that result in productivity rates lower than expected. In this view, the crisis of productivity and commitment is a problem of the skills and attitudes made possible and produced by work environments. The solutions advocated within this position have sometimes required altering the design of work processes, the structures of authority in the workplace, or both.

The activities in this chapter will help students to better understand how work environments affect the abilities and attitudes workers are able to demonstrate. Furthermore, they raise questions about the implications of this understanding for redefining what worker commitment and responsibility might mean. The point of these activities is not to condemn certain jobs and celebrate others; neither is it to encourage or discourage particular occupational decisions. Rather, it is to gain insight into the possibilities and limitations of work as experienced by people in the work force, and to move beyond the matter of "choosing" an occupation into a disucssion of how working life might be improved.

The activities contained in this chapter are:

- Activity One: Does work design matter?
- Activity Two: Rationalizing work
- Activity Three: The experience of workplace changes
- Activity Four: Is work rationalization always rational? What counts as a good day for you?
- Activity Five: Skills and social differences in the workplace

Activity One: Does Work Design Matter?

In this book we have taken the position that work design can affect the quality of working life. In other words, work design does matter. However, this position is not necessarily a commonplace understanding. The following activity will help students begin to recognize the issues at stake and the personal implications of job design.

What to Do in the Classroom

Drawing on the introduction to this chapter and general information available on the problem of productivity in our society, introduce students to the issue of the relations among work design, the opportunity to develop, maintain, and display skills, and workers' responses to work. Briefly explain the concept of productivity. Provide students with some basic information about why issues of productivity are important to a community and how productivity rates might be affected. Point out that the way low productivity rates are commonly understood is through an exclusive emphasis on worker performance, most often citing absenteeism, turnover, strikes, slowdowns, and lack of commitment to assigned tasks.

Ask for student views on whether and why they think worker performance is a problem in our country today. What are the reasons for this aspect of the crisis of productivity? Keep in mind the two views (lack of a proper work ethic versus poorly designed jobs) offered in the introduction and present them, along with the student responses, as possibilities that should be considered.

The concept of "job size" can raise important questions about the relation between people and their work. What is job size? Job descriptions often attempt to specify the knowledge, skills, and abilities required to do a particular job. Job descriptions differ from each other not only in terms of these requirements but also in the number, variety, and level of complexity of items specified in a description. Therefore, jobs (more precisely, job descriptions) can be compared in terms of the opportunities they provide for people to exercise their knowledge, skills, and abilities and the scope that they provide for the development and extension of the capacities people bring to their work. This comparison between jobs determines relative job size. Job size is directly affected by the way work in an organization is defined and distributed. The concept is cogently illustrated in the words of Nora Watson, an editor for a publishing company:

Jobs are not big enough for people. It's not just the assembly line worker whose job is too small for his spirit, you know? A job like mine, if you really put your spirit into it, you would sabotage immediately. You don't dare. So you absent your spirit from it. My mind has been so divorced from my job, except as a source of income, it's really absurd. (Nora Watson in Studs Terkel's *Working*. New York: Avon Books, 1972. p. 675.)

The following activities are based on the notion of job size and utilize the opportunity students have to investigate how work is accomplished in the situations in which they work.

A. After students have been at their workplaces for several weeks, ask them to write up job descriptions for themselves based on what they have actually been doing. Suggested categories for these descriptions are:

- what I need to *know about*
- what I need to *know how to do*
- what *tasks I perform*
- what I am *responsible for*

B. Make a copy of each student's job description for every member of the class (if this activity is to be done in small groups, try to keep the group size no smaller than seven or eight students; each student should get a copy of the descriptions written by all members of his or her group).

Briefly introduce and discuss the idea of job size, perhaps using the Nora Watson extract above as a catalyst for discussion. Distribute the descriptions and ask students to sort them into three piles, from the largest to the smallest, in terms of job size. Have students compare their sorts and discuss any disagreements. What will become evident in this discussion is that students' work placements vary in job size.

C. Ask students to explore why some of their jobs differ in size by considering the overall work environment, focusing particularly on the way work is organized and distributed. Have students consider how job size might influence their interest in doing a particular type of work and their understanding of what conditions might be necessary for that interest to be satisfied on the job.

Activity Two: Rationalizing Work

Job design and the definition of skills have historically been tied to a concern with efficiency. The following two suggestions help introduce students to the history and logic of work rationalization. Each suggestion is based on a short portrayal of how rationalization has entered a particular work environment. In discussing these portrayals one should help students consider possible contradictions between the desire for efficient job design and the actual productivity resulting from particular job arrangements.

A. Ford: Hero or Villain. Have students read the short description of Henry Ford's innovation in job design provided below. Ask students to debate whether Ford should be considered a hero or villain of the twentieth century.

B. Henry Leffingwell and the "Office of the Future." Have students read the short description of the transformation of office work. Ask students to consider whether this transformation has provided adequate benefits to justify its existence. Also have students consider whether or not the computerization of the office is different from or similar to the realization of Leffingwell's dream.

Teaching Note

The two portrayals have different implications for a consideration of how gender issues have entered the workplace. Teachers wanting to stress questions of gender and work equity may wish to place a priority on the text "Henry Leffingwell and the 'Office of the Future.' "

Henry Ford's Innovation

The Ford Motor Company was founded in 1903.[2] At that time, the task of building automobiles was reserved for "craftsmen" who had been trained in the bicycle and carriage trades. The job itself was highly skilled, with automobiles being assembled in one spot by teams of "all-around" mechanics. By 1908, the assembly process had changed somewhat. Specialization had begun and now several mechanics were responsible for each side of the automobile. As well, less skilled and lower paid "stock-runners" were responsible for supplying parts and tools to the mechanics. In 1914, Ford introduced the endless chain assembly line for the new Model T. Within three months assembly time was cut to one-tenth of what it was previously. With rationalization each worker on the line was responsible for one small, repetitive operation. Some installed fenders, others hung doors, and so on. As workers became accustomed to their jobs they became more skilled. Ford could double, then triple the rate of assembly. Formerly, under the piecework system, workers received a bonus for fast work and high productivity. Now tied to the production line pace, all workers received a flat rate of pay; in 1914 this was about $2.34 a day. The new technology was unpopular among workers and they quit in droves, partly because there were less mechanized, but highly paid auto assembly jobs still available in other plants. Faced with the problem of high turnover (300 percent in 1914) and the threat of unionization, Ford announced "the five-dollar day." By paying his workers double the prevailing rate, Ford solved both problems of turnover and unionization. Workers were now anxious to keep their jobs at Ford and those who couldn't keep up with the increased pace of work were easily replaced. Ford himself called the five-dollar day "the finest cost-cutting move we ever made." Other auto manufacturing plants had to follow Ford's example in order to compete, and eventually the pattern set at Ford became the manufacturing industry standard. Ford's innovation in job design has only recently been modified with the introduction of computer-driven robots into the auto assembly process.

Henry Leffingwell and the "Office of the Future"

In 1850, clerical workers made up less than 1 percent of the total work force.[3] By 1900, they accounted for between 3 and 4 percent. Today, better than 20 percent of the work force is classified as clerical. The greatest changes, aside from absolute numbers, have been in the gender composition of the clerical work force and the wage paid to clerical workers.

In 1850, women were less than one-tenth of 1 percent of the clerical work force. By 1900, 25 percent of clerical workers were women. Today, women make up about 80 percent of clerical occupations. This shift in composition of the clerical work force was accompanied by a corresponding shift in the relative status and pay given clerical workers. In 1850, clerical workers were in the top 10 percent of wage earners. Today, the median weekly wage of a clerical worker is lower than every type of blue-collar work. The only groups to earn less are service sector workers and farm laborers.

At one time the clerical worker was the managerial counterpart of the skilled craftsman, with ordinary clerks, copying clerks, and office boys serving as clerical apprentices. The work itself involved bookkeeping, time keeping, payroll, quality control, commercial traveling, drafting, copying by hand, preparing accounts, correspondence, filing, and so on. In large modern corporations these functions have become separate departments. Office managers, borrowing from industrial management theory and practice, have rationalized clerical work so that it comes more and more to resemble production work.

Part of the impetus for this change was the publication in 1917 of *Scientific Office Management* by William Henry Leffingwell. With the goal of efficient office reorganization in mind, Leffingwell used time and motion studies to reveal "useless time and wasted effort" in office work. To study stenographic and typing output, typewriters were equipped with mechanical devices to count strokes, which would be used as a basis for piecework payment. Typists would be paid for what they produced, as measured by the number of strokes they typed per day. This concern with efficiency, however, proved counterproductive in that typists never used tab keys (but always the space bar) to increase their count and their pay—in effect, slowing down production.

The efforts of *Scientific Office Management* were put into devising elaborate systems for recording the output of office workers in order to set minimum standards and raise average standards in an attempt to establish a "fair day's work." Office layout was also given an extraordinary amount of attention. Pneumatic tubes and conveyor belts came to symbolize the modern office. At one point, Leffingwell calculated the placement of water fountains in one particular office. The placement was such that each clerk walked an average of 100 feet for a drink, "causing workers in this office to walk 40,000 miles per year for water with a corresponding loss of time for the employer!" His solution was to place everything within each reach of the clerk, leaving no excuse for being away from the desk. As Henry Ford said, "Save ten steps a day for 12,000 employees and you will have saved 50 miles of wasted motion and misspent energy."

Misspent energy meant energy not directly spent in production for the employer. What is not calculated here is that such energy might be necessary for the physical and mental well-being of employees. What is not recognized, for example, is the physical and social context and significance of the walk to the water fountain. However, many workers and employers are now recognizing that the physical and mental well-being of the worker contributes to productivity—that the most technically efficient way to organize work is not necessarily the most productive. This has lead to the growing interest in "job enrichment," "quality of working life," and the "task of building commitment." It has caused managers and job design consultants to rethink rationalization and come up with alternative ways to redesign and reorganize work.

Activity Three: The Experience of Workplace Changes

A source of valuable information regarding workplace changes and how they have influenced the opportunities for workers to display skills is the longtime employee. The following is a suggestion on how students might learn from the experiences of older workers.

What to Do in the Classroom

Assign students the task of interviewing a longtime employee in order to assess changes in the nature of work and their impact on people. While students should participate in the formulation of a list of questions to be asked, we provide some suggestions here.

• How long have you worked in this field?
• How long have you worked in this company/organization?
• How long have you worked at this job?
• Has this job changed since you started working for this organization?
• Has it changed since you've been doing the job?
• How have these changes affected the skills needed to do this job?
• What have these changes meant for you and for other people doing this job? For example, has it made the job easier or harder, more challenging or less?
• Has the pay changed as a result of the changes?
• Did the changes require you or others to develop new capabilities and acquire new information?

Activity Four: Is Work Rationalization Always Rational? What Counts as a Good Day for You?

This activity will help students explore the ways that the logic of work rationalization may influence how people feel about their jobs. It allows students to uncover and consider the possible contradiction between the logic of task analysis and work design, and the lack of efficiencies that are their result. The activity is also designed to initiate discussion about how work processes might be reorganized and improved in a way that resolves such possible contradictions.

Work rationalization refers here to a procedure that subjects a given work process to a task analysis, divides that process into its component required tasks, and assigns workers to tasks in a manner intended to increase the productivity of that work process.

What to Do in the Classroom

A. Give students about 20 minutes to write:

1. About your work placement or part-time employment: where you work, what is done there, what you do, what others do around you.

2. About your best day at work so far: what you did from beginning to end, how you felt about what you did, why it was your best day.

3. About your worst day so far: what you did, how you felt about what you did, why it was your worst day.

B. Have students meet in groups of five or six for 30–40 minutes.

1. All students read what they have written to other members of the group, answering any questions raised by their statement.

2. Ask students to listen for commonalties, things that made for good and bad days across work sites and occupational groupings.

3. Generate a list of five features of "good" work and five features of "bad" work (not necessarily common to all). Have students give each other examples with specific details; for example, do not just describe work as "boring," but specify what was boring and why.

C. Make two lists on the board with the following headings: "Things that make work good" and "Things that make work not so good." Ask for one feature for either list from any group. Do other groups have anything similar? Combine overlapping ideas and refine terminology until both lists are done. Partial lists might look something like this:

Good	Bad
challenging	repetitive
meet people	bad weather
responsibility	isolation
what was expected	unpredictable
Fridays	Mondays
learned new things	unprepared
treated like adult	treated like a child
see results of work	oversupervised

D. Introduce the concept of rationalization. Does it help explain the difference between "good" and "bad" work? Are jobs that have been rationalized more likely to contain features of good or bad work? (Obviously, rationalization offers only a partial explanation. Having to work in bad weather is not attributable to the process.) Are features of good work threatened by rationalization? If so, which ones?

E. Use the two lists to initiate a discussion about things that could be done to make work better. How could work be reorganized to provide more of the good features and eliminate some of the bad features? The discussion could focus on the specifics of the student's job, his or her workplace more generally, or work in society. Are the recommendations for reorganization feasible? Why or why not? What are the barriers?

Teaching Note

The two lists generated could also be used to evaluate work as it is represented in interviews, literature, drama, music, and so on. This could be done by having students, while reading, watching, or listening to forms of expression that encompass reactions to work, focus on what kinds of things make work good, satisfying, and rewarding or boring, frustrating, and alienating.

Activity Five: Skills and Social Differences in the Workplace

In many workplaces, students will notice that different work (and different pay rates and opportunity for advancement) seems to be done by people according to differences in gender, race, ability, and age. While not all distributions of people to jobs are the result of inequitable practices, students should be given the opportunity to consider whether and how existing policies in work organizations maintain unequal divisions among people.

What to Do in the Classroom

Have students produce an organization chart of their workplace indicating which people hold which jobs. This activity can operate at two levels. Students can be asked to observe and record within their immediate work surroundings or can be directed to seek out information regarding the larger organization structure.

Have students examine the charts they produce. Ask them to consider if there are clear divisions based on ethnicity, age, gender, race, and ability/disability.

Having made these observations, ask students to see how different members of their workplace explain the existence of such divisions (or account for the absence of such divisions). The justifications recorded should then be brought back to class. Pose the question: Are any of these divisions justifiable? Follow this by having the class consider what would have to be done to overcome the divisions that are not.

It also should be pointed out that the very fact that people hold different positions in a workplace and do different jobs can, in and of itself, create a sense of social difference among people. In other words, social differences among people do not just exist before they enter the workplace, but the technical and social relations of the workplace also influence the production and maintenance of such differences. For example, manual workers may experience a sense of difference from office workers within the same organization, a difference that is continually reinforced by each worker's daily participation in different forms of technical relations. One way of drawing this to the students' attention is to ask students, on the basis of the organization charts recorded, to identify those whom they consider to be "co-workers." Then have students discuss whether or not they feel that they "belong with this group" (whether they feel accepted, and not someone "apart" from the others). Pursue this by raising questions concerning what factors contribute to this sense of belonging. How do the social and technical relations of the workplace anchor and support the production of difference?

NOTES

1. The notion of "productivity" is important for students to understand. It can be defined simply as how much a work force produces in a given period of time. More generally, it relates to cost per unit of production. Our concern here is with how much a worker produces in a period of time, not with the full range of complex ways of cost accounting a unit of production.

2. Harry Braverman, *Labor and Monopoly Capital: The Degradation of Work in the 20th Century* (New York: Monthly Review Press, 1974), pp. 139–52.

3. Ibid., pp. 293–358.

5

Teachers Working with Employers: Developing the Learning Potential of Work Sites

As we have stressed from the outset, we view student experience as central to a critical pedagogy of work education. Many of the suggestions made in this book presume that students will have had access to some form of work experience in either part-time work or in programs of planned work-study. As well, we have continually stressed the importance of rejecting the view that every work experience in and of itself is educationally beneficial or that experience simply "speaks for itself." On the contrary, we have emphasized throughout our commentary the importance of both the conceptual resources a student has for making sense of her or his experience and the features of the work process that structure the possibilities for learning available to students.

In this chapter we shall directly discuss what a teacher can do to help provide students with work sites that are rich in learning potential. This of course presumes some form of work-study arrangement in which the teacher will have some influence in determining the range of experiences made available to students. What we want to encourage is the recognition that in work education, teachers not only work directly with students but with employers as well. The discussion and suggestions of this chapter are aimed at helping teachers work with employers. More specifically, what we suggest is a framework that enables teachers to "read" work sites for their learning potential and provide a basis for deliberating with both employers and students with regard to how learning might be enhanced in a given workplace.

Practitioners in work-study education tend to concentrate their efforts on finding "good sites" and then monitoring students to ensure that no problems arise. Yet what counts as a "good" site often remains unclear. Understanding more about the process of on-the-job learning can enable teachers to take a more active role in developing the educational potential of a workplace. By having some understanding of the circumstances under which certain kinds of on-the-job learning experiences are likely to occur, teachers may begin to extend their pedagogical practice from the classroom into the workplace. This is not simply rhetoric. What is suggested here is the development of a capability for giving direction and support to employers participating in work-study programs by making explicit to them the kinds of activities and ways of working with students that are likely to enhance their learning experiences. It is to this end that we provide the following framework for understanding learning at work.

UNDERSTANDING LEARNING AT WORK

A useful framework for analyzing the experiences of students in work-study programs has been developed by David Moore in the context of his research on student workplace learning. Moore's work assumes that work sites can usefully be viewed as settings in which interactions among people are organized through particular conceptions of purpose, meanings, roles, and events. Furthermore, he assumes that in such settings new members will have to use such work-site features to develop a sense of competence—a sense of "working knowledge." In other words, Moore begins with questions of what students need to know and how they come to know it. He writes:

From an educational perspective, our central problem was to discover and analyze the social process by which the newcomer to the workplace was more or less systematically introduced into the definition, distribution, and use of knowledge [necessary to do one's job].[1]

The curricular content of a student's work experience is comprised of knowledge about the technical and social relations that organize production processes at her or his workplace. Technical relations refer to the tools, machines, technology, processes, work flow, and technical knowledge utilized in the production of goods or the provision of services. Social relations refer to the relations of workers to each other and to management. It is the social and technical relations of production that define the work situation made manifest in a particular organization of tasks.

For Moore, the process of learning at work begins when students are integrated into the task activities of the work site, that is, when students begin to participate in some portion of the ongoing, productive work in which others at the workplace are engaged. It is through the observation and performance of tasks that students come to understand the nature and use of the working knowledge required of workers. As well, Moore's focus on tasks provides a unit of analysis that reveals aspects of work situations that offer the possibility for pedagogical intervention. To understand how a consideration of tasks might be of pedagogical value, consider how Moore defines the features of tasks in a work environment.

Logical-Technical and Pragmatic Task Features

Moore identifies the logical-technical features of tasks as the knowledge and skill required of workers to "get the job done" in a way that demonstrates competence to fellow workers. These features represent one aspect of the shared definition and use of knowledge in the workplace. The logical-technical features of tasks may be related to manual or physical skills (changing a tire, bathing a patient) or cognitive skills (reading a blueprint, designing a logo). They may also include relational or affective skills (chatting with a client, comforting a child). In many instances, these logical-technical features are what are emphasized in the training profiles developed for commonly used occupational placements.

Another crucial feature of tasks, however, is the meaning they have both for individuals and for groups within the social context of the workplace. Moore calls these features "pragmatic." The organizational significance of any given task can be determined relative to its position in the production process. A task can be central or peripheral to the work process; a task can be dependent on the work of others or the work of others can be dependent on it; a task can have high visibility and recognition or it can be part of the "invisible," largely unrecognized work of a business, institution, or agency. Individuals ascribe meanings to tasks that may be consistent or at variance with their organizational significance. Performance of some tasks might be clearly associated with certain levels of status or prestige in the workplace. Working directly with children, for example, is seen to carry more status than preparation of materials in a daycare center; cutting material carries more status than stripping furniture in an upholstery shop. There may, however, be other considerations in determining the pragmatic significance of a task. For the novice or student a routine task like typing a letter or sharpening a drill bit might be seen as an occasion to demonstrate a level of proficiency that could lead to more interesting or important work. These same tasks, however, might well be understood as boring or demeaning "joe jobs" if their connection to productive or "real" work is ambiguous.

In thinking about the curricular content of students' work experiences, it is important to recognize the pragmatic as well as the logical-technical features of tasks. Learning the job entails an understanding of both the technical and social relations that define the production process. In other words, in addition to learning to *do* work, students should learn something *about* the work they are doing and the context in which they are doing it.

Learning with Task Episodes

While task features specify what knowledge can be learned on a job, they do not specify how it is that a student may have access to such knowledge. Taking into account the social organization of personnel, information, and material necessary for students to accomplish certain tasks at work, Moore proposes a framework for understanding the "pedagogy of work experience" based on what he calls "task episodes." This framework provides a way of conceptualizing the social process by which a student encounters a task, works on it, and receives feedback regarding her or his performance. In other words, task episodes detail how learners gain access to various segments of the working knowledge of a work site.

To illustrate some of the ways in which people in work settings enact the three phases of task episodes, Moore uses the following examples:

1. Modes of encountering a task
   a. show and tell: supervisor performs the task while talking about it, showing students how to do it
   b. sink or swim: supervisor assigns student to perform task without giving explicit instructions ("Just go do it!")
   c. self-starting: student decides to undertake particular task
2. Modes of accomplishing a task
   a. following the script: student performs task according to guidelines established earlier by supervisor
   b. playing it by ear: student does what seems necessary and right, without explicit guidelines
   c. taking plays from the sidelines: student performs task with continual coaching from supervisor
3. Modes of evaluating performance and accessing feedback
   a. coaching: supervisor gives continuous feedback and guidance during performance, suggesting strategies and techniques
   b. formal supervision: after the performance, supervisor meets with student to review quality of performance, suggests improvements
   c. testing the product: student checks to see if the product of the performance works.[2]

These examples are neither exhaustive nor mutually exclusive. Rather, they represent a range in the patterned activity through which tasks are established, accomplished, and evaluated. To the extent that these aspects of a task episode determine students' access to the working knowledge of the work site, they shape the learning potential of that work site for the student. Furthermore, the task episodes available to the student will also influence the degree to which she or he becomes integrated into the production process and initiated into the culture of the workplace. This in turn influences the total quality of students' on-the-job learning experiences.

A Learning Trajectory

Of course one should not expect that the task features and episodes that engage students will remain the same during the entire course of a work placement. To avoid the static quality of simple task analysis, Moore extends his framework to include changes over time in both the tasks students undertake and in the means by which tasks are established, accomplished, and evaluated. This allows a way of gauging the progress of the learning process on the job. In this respect the following types of questions might be asked:

- Do tasks become more demanding and complex in a logical-technical sense, requiring more in the way of physical, cognitive, or relational skills?
- Do tasks become more important in a pragmatic sense? Are they a "real" part of the ongoing work process? Do they lead to more interesting or valued work?
- Is there a move toward more independence in the means by which tasks are established? Can the student negotiate the terms of the task? Is the student more able to initiate tasks?
- Does the student become more aware of the human and material resources available for accomplishing a task? Does the organizational context of the production process become better understood by the student?
- Does direct supervision occur less frequently? Is the student able to evaluate her or his own performance? Does the student develop a sense of competence and knowledgeability? Is the student given more responsibility?

It should be obvious at this point that the extent and quality of students' learning over time, what Moore calls the "trajectory" of learning, is related not only to the quality of the student's performance of specific tasks, but also to the nature of the tasks themselves and the ongoing work processes within which they are embedded. By taking into account task features and task episodes, Moore's framework allows us to analyze how the social and technical relations of production contribute to or inhibit the trajectory of a student's on-the-job learning experiences. This kind of understanding provides a basis upon which to assess the learning potential of a given work site. It helps us to identify requisite knowledges, skills, and abilities (logical-technical features), recognize the organizational and individual significance of tasks (pragmatic features), and take into account the social means by which students are initiated into the practices and underlying knowledge-in-use of the workplace. Moreover, because the analysis focuses on such practices, it provides teachers with a framework for working with employers to develop plans and procedures that will contribute to students' learning.

APPLYING THE FRAMEWORK: AN EXAMPLE

To help clarify the utility of Moore's framework for developing the learning potential of work sites, consider the following example drawn from our own research on the determination of student experiences within cooperative education programs. Two students from the same class were placed in different hairdressing salons for an extended cooperative education work placement. Their co-op program required them to be at work from nine in the morning to three in the afternoon for ten weeks. In workplace observations and employee/employer interviews it was noted that one of these students spent a considerable amount of time drinking coffee and looking at magazines while the other student was typically more involved in the routine work of the salon, that is, cleaning the shop, shampooing customers, and assisting the operators. A close look at some of the task features and episodes of the practices in these two salons is helpful in understanding what made these two students' experiences and learning trajectories so different. As will be seen, this is an understanding that goes beyond ascribing these differences to individual student "initiative," taking into account those pedagogical features of work processes that a teacher or employer is able to do something about.

There is a wide variety of tasks available to students in a hairdressing salon. These include: answering the phone and making appointments; sweeping the floor; washing and folding towels; running errands; shampooing customers; and helping the operators by neutralizing perms, combing out sets, blow-drying, braiding, and so on. By law, students are not permitted to cut or color hair and therefore have no real clients or customers themselves. In a logical-technical sense, the range of available tasks provides ample opportunity for students to develop some of the knowledge, skills, and abilities required of a hairdresser. To the extent that students are able to participate in the full range of available tasks, they can become more proficient in the tools of the trade and more knowledgeable about the day-to-day operations of a salon and the technical procedures involved in working with clients' hair. Not to be underestimated (and perhaps most importantly), performance of tasks and participation in the work process enables the student to develop an understanding of the social relations that shape hairdressing as a production process. The ability to talk with customers, to establish rapport, and to help create an atmosphere or ambience is important not just for the salon, but for the hairdresser trying to build up a clientele. The ability to get along with other operators is vital in a situation where the pace of work is so erratic. During slow periods operators have only each other to talk to; during peak periods they must rely on each other for help. The occupation is also characterized by a complex set of interrelated gender, authority, and exchange relations. The work process is embedded in these structures of social relations and access to the working knowledge of the site is dependent on participation in these relations of production.

In Moore's pragmatic sense, the tasks available to students (especially those tasks that can be performed with little or no supervision) are not central to the work process. While they often are essential to the smooth operation of the salon (clean towels are important, and so is coffee) the tasks themselves generally carry no status or prestige. Moreover, limiting students to those tasks that can be performed independently, such as answering the phone, sweeping up, running errands, or washing towels, effectively blocks their participation in what are probably the most important sets of social relations and work practices—those between an operator and customer and among operators themselves. It is in the context of helping the operator that the student is most able to learn and to demonstrate competence in terms of technical skills and relational abilities. Because participation in the real work of the salon—cutting hair—is not an option for students, helping the operator becomes the only means of gaining access to the hairdresser's knowledge-in-use. As well, helping the operator recontextualizes the routine tasks students typically perform. The pragmatic significance of these tasks shifts from "helping in the salon" to "helping the operators." For the operators too, the performance of routine tasks is seen less as "doing what's expected" and more as "really helping us out."

The differences in the two hairdressing students' experiences can be partially explained in terms of differences in task episodes, that is, by differences in the way tasks in the salons were established, accomplished, and evaluated. In one salon, the student was generally assigned those kinds of tasks for which she was presumed already to be competent. With minimal or no direction, she could run an errand, answer the phone, sweep the floor, fold towels, or shampoo a customer. When she wasn't performing such routine tasks, she was expected to observe what was going on in the shop. For her this meant sitting and watching and waiting for someone to tell her to do something else. She did not want to get in the way and assumed that if someone needed help, they would ask for it. The problem with this assumption is that operators, accustomed to working on clients alone, don't often need help. Unless the responsibility to enlist help is explicit, the operator is likely to carry on as usual. In this instance, the operators expected the student to volunteer, to come to them and ask, "Can I help?". When she didn't, they took her timidity as a sign of indifference, as a lack of enthusiasm and initiative. Over the course of her work placement, the tasks this student was given remained essentially the same. There was no change in the level of her participation in the everyday life of the salon. In Moore's terms, her learning trajectory remained flat. Her placement provided only minimal access to the knowledge-in-use in a hairdressing salon.

In the second salon, the task of helping the operators was much more explicit. Operators understood that this student was in the salon not just to clean up and observe, but to learn something about hairdressing. They felt responsible (some more than others) for teaching this student something and regularly invited her participation in their work. The limitations on what kinds of things the student was able to do remained the same (no cutting, no chemicals) but the 'place' of the student in the salon was fundamentally different. Not only was the onus of responsibility for initiating these helping-out tasks not presumed to be the student's alone, but it was assumed by each of the operators in the salon. As a result the student was able to develop and display some of the manual, cognitive, and relational skills that lead to a more complete integration into the everyday life of the salon. This included but was not limited to work process-related tasks. While this student was certainly permitted to do more "real" work on customers' heads (setting, combing out, neutralizing, blow-drying), participation in these helping-out tasks also enabled her to learn more about the life of a hairdresser and hairdressing as an occupation. The perils of opening a salon, the drawbacks of working in franchises, the importance of developing a clientele, the reasons for entering competitions—these and other topics and issues became part of her developing understanding of the kind of work she intended to pursue. Her learning trajectory can be described as a rising curve, with the student becoming not only more technically competent but also more occupationally knowledgeable.

Both of these salons had the potential to be interesting and useful work sites. The tasks available to students were basically the same. The relation of tasks to work processes and to knowledge-in-use afforded the same opportunities for students to participate in, and hence gain an understanding of, the technical and social relations that organized the work of the salon. The different experiences of the two students, however, serves as a reminder that the process of learning on the job involves more than placing students in potentially rich environments. Access to knowledge depends on enabling their active participation in the practices of these work sites. As Moore points out:

The central educational question in the workplace is not whether rich forms of knowledge are in use in the environment, but rather whether and how new-comers like interns get access to that knowledge: how they encounter it, take it in, are called upon to display it, get to work on it and even transform it.[3]

Because participation is so crucial it should not be left to chance, employer discretion, or student initiative. The terms of the work-study agreement should be such that they ensure the opportunity for students to participate in a full range of tasks. Over the course of the work placement the student should become involved in tasks that are more complex and more demanding in a logical-technical sense. Pragmatically, the tasks should become more important, more central to the ongoing work of the work site. Moreover, the social means for establishing, accomplishing, and evaluating tasks should move in the direction of greater actual participation (less observation) and more independence (less supervisory intervention). These expectations should be spelled out and clearly understood by supervising teachers, employers and employees, and students at the start of any work-study placement.

In the following activities, Moore's framework will be applied to the development of student training profiles and evaluation forms. As well, the concepts will be related to the process of monitoring students on a work site. The activities are intended to provide teachers with some practical suggestions for analyzing the curricular content and pedagogical practices of the work placements they use. Recognizing the factors that contribute to the process of on-the-job learning will enable teachers to make sure that these factors are understood by employers and manifest in the forms used to plan, record, and assess work experiences.

WORKING WITH EMPLOYERS: ACTIVITIES

In the preceding pages we have set out a conceptual framework for describing and analyzing features of work that contribute to or inhibit the process of on-the-job learning. This second section uses that framework to address three specific areas of teacher/employer collaboration: (1) the development of training profiles and training plans; (2) monitoring student performance; and (3) student evaluation.

In many jurisdictions, school board or community college-approved forms are used to specify the kinds of activities that will be available to students in a work site and the criteria against which their performance will be evaluated. For this reason, it is important to ensure that the forms

used include features that reflect a conceptualized and dynamic understanding of the process of on-the-job learning. Contained in this section,
therefore, are recommendations for developing conceptually consistent
formats and procedures for describing, recording, and evaluating the
quality of a student's work experience. Discussing these forms and procedures with employers and participating with them in the processes of
planning, monitoring, and evaluation will enable teachers to give support and direction to employers by making explicit the kinds of activities
and ways of establishing, accomplishing, and evaluating tasks that are
likely to enhance students' learning.

Activity One: Training Profiles and Training Plans

The challenge in developing a good training profile is to explicate the
full range of learning possibilities that might be available to students at
a work site. This requires thinking beyond the category of "jobs" and
technical skills required to do them and recognizing that all workplaces
can provide the opportunity for students to learn about (by participating
in) the complex social and technical relations that organize production
processes. This is why it is so important that the training profile be
comprehensive and include learning objectives related to improving specific skills, increasing occupational knowledge, and developing relational
and affective abilities. Moreover, the profile should be explicit about
what students will actually do to accomplish these objectives. Statements
like "the student will observe what's going on and help out where
needed" do little to ensure that the student won't be locked into the
performance of routine tasks that provide little opportunity for learning.
Task statements that are precise and sequenced to reflect increasing
levels of complexity, however, convey a sense of commitment to the
process of on-the-job learning and set out clear expectations for learning
trajectories.

Objectives

In developing an occupational training profile or modifying an existing
profile, one of the first questions to ask is: Is this profile comprehensive?
Do the tasks or activities address all the logical-technical demands of
the occupation? Are there tasks or activities designed to improve the
student's manual or physical skills? Are there tasks or activities that will
lead to increased knowledge and understanding of work processes and
procedures? Are there tasks or activities that will enable the student to
develop relational and affective abilities?

One way to make sure that these areas are addressed is to organize
the profile in such a way that these logical-technical features become
stated learning objectives. For example, a teacher might begin by stating

that a student will: "develop proficiency in the use of materials, tools, and equipment commonly found in an automotive shop"; or "develop an understanding of the work processes and procedures in a travel agency"; or "develop the ability to work with and relate to co-workers, supervisors, and patients in a hospital ward." For educators who are committed to a form of education that includes thinking about work and not merely doing it, these kinds of statements of purpose are quite important. Being explicit about learning objectives that cover both intentions ensures that the workplace will be recognized as a site that offers a range of potential learning experiences that extend beyond specific skills training.

Tasks

Listed under each of the statements of purpose would be the tasks, activities, and opportunities afforded the student that are most likely to achieve an intended objective. While it is true that some tasks will serve more than one objective, the point is to make sure that each learning objective related to some aspect of the development of working knowledge, skills, and abilities is addressed in the training profile. The tasks listed under learning objectives can convey a sense of why the tasks are being performed. They should be written in such a way as to describe as clearly as possible what the student is expected or permitted to do— that is, how the student will accomplish the task. The task statement should also identify the material, information, and human resources to be utilized in the accomplishment of the task. While it is not our intent here to belabor the issue of how to write a task description, the following is provided as a brief illustration.

1. *Objective*: "The student will develop proficiency in the use of materials, tools, and equipment commonly found in an automotive shop."

   Such tasks might include:
   - use of wire brush valves to remove carbon buildup
   - removing and sandblasting spark plugs
   - removing and replacing rocker cover
   - installing rings on pistons
   - installing oil pans

2. *Objective*: "The student will develop knowledge and understanding of engine and power train maintenance and repair."

   Such tasks might include:
   - assisting master mechanic with compression test
   - assisting master mechanic with vacuum test
   - assisting master mechanic with removal and replacement of clutch

- assisting master mechanic with removal and replacement of transmission and differential
3. *Objective*: "The student will develop the ability to work with and relate to co-workers, supervisors, and customers of the shop."

  Such tasks might include:

- picking up and delivering parts
- delivering vehicles to customers
- eating lunch with co-workers
- "job shadowing" a supervisor
- attending a meeting of the Occupational Health and Safety Committee

Tasks listed under each learning objective need not follow a strict sequential organization. They should, however, convey a sense of development; that is, movement from simple to more complex and demanding tasks (and task sets) should be readily apparent on the training profile itself. The sequence of task statements should also reflect changes in the social means whereby tasks are accomplished. As students become more knowledgeable and proficient, observing and assisting tasks should give way to actual performance tasks. This shift in the language of task accomplishment indicates a clear expectation that students gradually become more and more integrated into the actual ongoing work of the site. The exception to this pattern of increased responsibility and actual performance is the situation in which a student is not able or permitted to do a particular kind of task for pragmatic or regulatory reasons (e.g., students would not be expected to supervise a department; neither would they be permitted to evaluate a patient, cut a customer's hair, etc.). Still, their experiences should not be limited only to those kinds of tasks they are able to perform independently. Because the workplace offers the opportunity for students to become not only technically more proficient but also occupationally more knowledgeable, students should be involved in a full range of tasks, including supervisory tasks, even though their participation might be limited to observing and assisting.

The Individual Training Plan

The individual training plan codifies and formalizes the terms and conditions under which the student will participate in the activities of the workplace. Insofar as the training plan directs students' participation it is crucial that the teacher ensure that the plan itself emphasizes the process of on-the-job learning, and that the plan and the process are well understood by students and workplace personnel. Although final responsibility for developing the training plan is the teacher's, clarity of purpose and of process is enhanced when both students and workplace personnel are involved in preparing the plan. It is in this sense that the plan is individual, taking into account both the interests and expectations of the student and the range of opportunities available in specific work sites.

The basic structure of the training plan is the same as that of the training profile, with stated learning objectives and a related sequence of tasks. The scope of the plan will not necessarily be as broad as the profile, owing to student differences and site specifics. However, the individual plan might include additional elements that reflect a particular student's interests or a unique work opportunity. The profile, in other words, provides the starting point for negotiating the terms and conditions of the work experience. Looking at the range of possibilities set out in the profile, the teacher, the student, the employer, and the training supervisor can select from and add to the objectives and related sets of activities in order to formulate a coherent and clearly defined training plan.

Although it is necessary to be explicit about what students will be expected to do and about how that "doing" should become more complex and connected to all aspects of the actual work of the workplace, this does not go far enough in ensuring that learning is emphasized at the training station. In addition, therefore, the training plan should include indicators of the social means whereby tasks are established and processed. If the workplace is seen as providing the opportunity for students to develop a sense of responsibility and initiative as well as technical proficiency, then these features should be manifest in the training plan—not as personality traits (e.g., "student demonstrates responsibility: Y/N") but as conceptualized abilities that the social relations of the workplace can foster or inhibit. One strategy for incorporating these features into the training plan would be to set out a continuum of social means for the establishment and processing of tasks. These continua would replace the common practice of leaving a space to "check off" that a task was performed and provide more in the way of describing the specifics of the circumstances under which the task was performed and how the performance might have changed over time. An example, of such a continuum might look something like this:

The student was given the opportunity to:
1. be told what to do and shown how to do it
2. be told what to do but left to own devices
3. self-initiate the task

Such a continuum signals the expectation that students will be given the opportunity to develop initiative and also allows for a more dynamic recording of students' workplace experiences. Note that although a task might be performed several times in the course of a placement, the means by which the task is established could (and should) change.

In a similar fashion, the training plan could incorporate other continua, reflecting, for instance, the way performance was reviewed and evaluated.

The student's performance of this task was:

1. continuously monitored

2. reviewed regularly

3. presumed to be competent

Once again this format signals the expectation that students will be given the opportunity to become more competent and more responsible. And, although a task might be performed several times, the means by which the task is processed could change over time to reflect increasing levels of competence and responsibility.

Activity Two: Monitoring

Effective student monitoring is a crucial, though somewhat under-utilized, means of promoting the process of learning on the job. Monitoring is most commonly understood as a combination of "trouble shooting," public relations, and program development. However, the monitoring process is sometimes seen as an intrusion into the work component of work-study programs. Attempting to reduce monitoring time at the workplace to a minimum often leads to an overemphasis on trouble shooting and PR at the expense of program development. In this section we propose that program development be established as the core of the monitoring process on the assumption that these other aspects can be effectively dealt with in the context of a program development process. In the interest of program development, the training plan becomes the central focus not only of initial discussions with employers and training station supervisors but also of subsequent monitoring visits.

Initial Contact and Discussions

Prior to the student's first day at work, employers should know that they will be expected to provide students with an orientation to the workplace. This orientation should include: health and safety regulations and procedures; workplace rules regarding such things as dress, absence, lateness, and so on; hours of work, lunch, break times; a tour of the company and introduction to facilities and personnel. These initial discussions should be seen as an occasion to examine the training profile and to establish with the employer and training station supervisor what kinds of things are possible given the particulars of their workplace. This information, together with information provided by the student, forms the basis on which the teacher can put together a preliminary draft of the individual training plan. This plan should be explicit enough to provide a sense of direction for both student and supervisor, but should also be understood as an evolving document to be modified and adjusted in the course of the placement if and when required. At the end of this initial period of contact, however, teacher, student, and workplace personnel should be clear about and in agreement with a fairly detailed short-term plan, which will be examined, discussed, and extended as part of the following monitoring visit.

Ongoing Visits and Discussions

Although students may or may not have been included in initial contacts and discussions with employers and supervisors, in most circumstances it makes good pedagogical sense for teachers, supervisors, and students to discuss the training plan together in subsequent monitoring visits. These discussions provide the opportunity to review student activities relative to the learning objectives set out in the training plan, to revise those objectives when necessary, and to develop a program of activities that builds on and extends what has already been accomplished. For example, the plan might indicate that the student has been involved in a wide variety of tasks with varying degrees of complexity and yet his or her level of participation in those tasks has not moved much beyond observing and helping. The strategy then might be to emphasize increased participation in fewer tasks for the next while. Conversely, the plan might indicate that the student has been given the opportunity not only to perform but to initiate a limited number of routine tasks. Here the recommendation might be to involve the student in a greater variety of tasks, although the level of participation might be reduced.

The content, form, and organization of the training plan recommended enables teachers, students, and supervisors to recognize several significant dimensions that contribute to the process of on-the-job learning. These include variety and complexity of tasks, degree of participation and involvement, and opportunity to develop and demonstrate both initiative and responsibility. To the extent that these dimensions are recognized and recorded, action can be taken to modify a program of activities in order to ensure that students are provided with the breadth and depth of experience necessary to make their participation in the workplace worthwhile. Because the teacher is, in the end, accountable for the quality of a student's work placement, it is essential that the program development potential of monitoring be fully utilized. To this end, the training plan conceptualized as an evolving document that sets out the terms and conditions of students' workplace participation is an invaluable tool.

Activity Three: Evaluation

A comprehensive training plan organized along the lines suggested here provides a coherent and consistent basis for the evaluation of students' learning on the job. Insofar as the plan is a statement of learning objectives and a record of activities and means of accomplishing those objectives, at the end of a placement the training plan documents student learning relative to a set of expectations agreed on and understood by everyone involved. Unlike checklists of generic "personal characteristics," which too often emphasized student demeanor, use of the training plan in evaluation links learning to opportunity in such a way that students are assessed on the basis of what they've done (and have been allowed to do) and how they've done it. This is not to ignore work habits and attitudes but rather to recognize that these qualities are context-dependent and must not be evaluated only as abstracted or essential personal characteristics. The implicit (though sometimes unrecognized) assumption that underlies characteristics-based evaluation—that is, that the students have been given the opportunity to develop and demonstrate initiative, responsibility, cooperation, and so on—is more explicit in the approach outlined in this unit. Moreover, this approach conveys the sense that the work site is most appropriately viewed as a place for students to learn, rather than a "testing ground" for their personalities.

NOTES

1. David Moore, "Learning at Work: Case Studies in Non-School Education," *Anthropology and Education Quarterly*, 17 (September 1986):167.

2. David Moore, "Discovering the Pedagogy of Experience," *Harvard Educational Review*, 51 (1981):295–96. See also: David Moore, *Working Knowledge: Toward a Conception of the Curriculum of Experience*, unpublished manuscript (New York University, April 1984).

3. Moore, "Learning at Work," p. 183.

III

Exploring Social Relations

6

Working Through Social Relations

And then the second day I went . . . I'd sort of like watched the day before, so I know what the routine was. . . . They'd be drawing like they were today, and sometimes the paper has, like, blue lines on the other side, because it's just like a scrap paper that they get. And the kids would turn them over and start scribbling. And then I'd be right beside them and she'd go: "No, don't do that." Like to the kid. And I wouldn't know, because she never did tell me. And I'm sort of going: "Oh." And I feel stupid because I'm watching the kid and I didn't know that they weren't allowed to draw on the other side of the page. And it's just, quite a few times that that's happpened. . . . She just does it and I'm supposed to sort of click in and see what she's doing . . . because she never tells me, you know. And I always just figure out stuff myself.

(Jennifer at a daycare center)

Clicking in . . . figuring stuff out. What does "fitting in" to a new work environment entail? Clearly, as Jennifer's experiences indicate, it is not just a matter of knowing the daily routines of the workplace and the practical ordering of tasks and activities. It is also a matter of establishing oneself as competent within preferred ways of doing things and within an existing range of social practices. Preferred ways of doing things are accomplished through relations of authority that often exclude students from establishing their sense of responsibility for their own actions. As a result, students often have to contend with experiences of self-doubt and of feeling ineffectual.

For many students, like Jennifer, making sense of such preferred workplace practices, deciding which ones matter, and whether or not to comply with them, can be a difficult process. Most importantly, it calls up ethical and political questions about the necessity of adapting to workplace conventions when these are seen to contradict students' own sense of what is fair and desirable. Is "clicking in," for example, a matter of conforming to work practices that already exist? Can it be consistent with questioning these practices for what they limit and circumscribe? Under what circumstances are challenges to workplace authority appropriate? How, and on what grounds, can students come to legitimate their own sense of the correct way to do things? How can they negotiate the contradictory demands of "being adaptable" and "taking risks" in ways that enable them to better participate in the determination of their working lives?

UNDERSTANDING SOCIAL RELATIONS

Worksites, as we have noted previously, are places where a sense of identity is confirmed, shaped, and contested. In this chapter we focus specifically on the ways in which *social relations at work* are implicit in this process, and how they serve to define and constrain what employers and employees value as initiative and competence. The concept of social relations is tricky. We often think of social relations simply as the way people relate to each other. However, for our purposes in this chapter, we need to expand on this notion. First, how people relate to each other is shaped by the way work is organized within a given context. This means seeing how the daily activities of workers are accomplished through such forms of organization as the division of labor; the allocation of time, space, and resources; and lines of responsibility and influence. Second, how people relate to each other is shaped by the relations of power these forms of organization bring into play—relations of power such as gender, race, age, class, and ability/disability. These relations of power help establish particular patterns of work practices in the workplace. Hence, the way people relate to each other at work must be seen as doubly organized.

It is within this double organization of the social and power relations of work that certain capacities are valued over others. It is also within this organization of relations at work that students come to define and confront responsibilities, constraints, and opportunities. Importantly, social relations at work are therefore never static, prescriptive, or neutral. Rather, they are sets of activities through which certain preferred ways of doing things and taken-for-granted assumptions are continually produced and reproduced. This means taking into account by whom and in whose interests such preferred knowledge is established. How people relate to each other in the workplace is therefore not simply a matter of personality, but also of how work gets done. And how work gets done is organized through a range of social relations that place people differently in relations of power.

Consider, for example, Jennifer's conflict with her supervisor. Like most students, Jennifer wants to be taken seriously as a competent and contributing member of the workplace. However, as she says above, she found herself in a situation that made her feel stupid and inadequate. Her initial way of making sense of this experience was to blame her supervisor for being unreasonable. This tendency to explain conflicts as the result of irrationality or mean-spiritedness is quite common at all levels of the workplace, and is a view that can be both limited and limiting. The importance of considering social relations at work is that it provides an alternative perspective to such judgments.

What does this mean in Jennifer's situation? Jennifer is confused and angry that she was not given adequate information about the routines and practices of the daycare center and her anger is not totally unwarranted. Her supervisor intervened in her working relation with a child without telling Jennifer why she had done so, leaving Jennifer feeling that she had done something wrong in not enforcing a rule she had not known about and did not understand. Her anger thus was obviously focused on the personality of her supervisor. Yet the genesis of this problem may lie elsewhere. The chronic underfunding, for example, of most daycare centers creates working conditions that are often not conducive to a continuous concern with helping new personnel grasp the way things are done. Lack of sufficient equipment and play activities can produce a constant demand on the adults present to continuously monitor child behavior, leaving little time and energy for explanations. If this is, at least in part, a plausible explanation of what is at play in Jennifer's situation, she then may begin to see that her anger might be directed not just at her supervisor but at the work practices that have shaped the relations between her and her supervisor. In this light, new questions can be asked and different issues addressed in an attempt to alter the supervisory relationship.

But there is even more at stake here. Without access to a relationship within which Jennifer can, with a sense of security and confidence, begin to ask questions concerning the way things are done in her workplace, it is unlikely she will be able to claim a position of responsibility vis-à-vis her actions there. Without such a possibility she remains without a degree of agency in negotiating how she would "fit in"—that is, how and if she can find a place in existing or perhaps modified work practices.

A pedagogy that helps students to see beyond personality conflicts as the sole cause of problems in workplace relations cannot be naive about the degree to which students (or even new employees) may challenge existing practices. This pedagogical focus may or may not help students resolve particular instances of misunderstanding and conflict. However, the view offered in this chapter is that seeing social relations in a new light will provide the grounds for alternative modes of action. Having access to such alternatives will better enable students to define the terms of their participation in working life.

This chapter is organized differently from most of the chapters in this book. The suggested classroom activities provide a number of student stories about social relations at work which may serve as vehicles for case study. Related discussion questions are provided both throughout the following sections and at the end of each case. The student stories are organized to reflect issues of social convention, initiative, authority, and identity as they are accomplished across a variety of work sites. These issues are treated in short thematic discussions that are intended to serve as resources for questions that teachers may wish to raise with their students. In order to ground these discussions as much as possible in actual experiences of students at work, we have drawn on interview material gathered during our extensive research on cooperative education programs.

This chapter is comprised of two sections.

- Section one: Thematic discussions:
  1. Social conventions at work
  2. Showing and taking initiative
  3. Authority at work
  4. Taking up an identity
- Section two: Student stories and discussion questions
  1. Daycare center
  2. Machine shop
  3. Fast food counter
  4. Radio station
  5. Family restaurant
  6. Residence for the elderly

SECTION ONE: THEMATIC DISCUSSIONS

Theme 1: Social Conventions at Work

As soon as Carol came into the salon, we knew that we had to do something to her right away because just, ah, you know, to fix her up, to make her look like, you know, she's part of the environment.

(Carol's supervisor at a hairdressing salon)

Social conventions at the workplace form sets of patterned activities and preferred ways of doing things that are often tacitly understood by workers in the daily practice of going about their work. Such conventions as dress codes, lunch and coffee-break times, control over public and private space, subjects of conversation, use of jargon, and fooling around on the job are practices through which social relations of difference, belonging, and the ability to feel at home in the workplace are continually organized and negotiated. Workplace conventions are one of the ways in which social relations become apparent as forms of regulation that support particular interests and lines of authority on the job.

The apparent "naturalness" of social conventions at work, and the perception that they are uniformly accepted by all workers, raise two kinds of questions. First, given that many students speak of themselves as being shy and afraid to make mistakes, how do they, as new workers, even begin to feel a part of social conventions at work? Second, if they do come to feel a part of things, how might this in turn produce a complicity in taken-for-granted ways of being in the workplace that precludes alternative visions and understandings of how one might be at work? In other words, the question is not just how to fit in, but also what newcomers are being asked to fit in to.

In the above excerpt, for example, some of the ambiguities of fitting in are brought to light. The supervisor saw his salon as a trendy and stylish place that catered to a youthful clientele; the style and personal appearance of those working in the salon were therefore important. Carol's "image," however, clearly did not match the preferred standards and expectations and she was consequently made over to fit in better. Indeed, the supervisor had her hair style and color changed, and suggested that she wear different clothes and make-up. Further, it was assumed that she too would find this change of image desirable, and that it would assist her in integrating into the workplace.

Expectations about personal appearance can be, and often are, contradictory for women in the workplace. Fitting in with the desired image at the salon, for example, can mean simultaneously complying with wider social and cultural conventions about what is appropriate to feminine style and fashion. Such conventions, because they are organized within relations of gender (themselves relations of power and authority) can, for some women, unjustly limit their participation in the workplace. Taken-for-granted ways of thinking about what counts as an "attractive" woman can reproduce traditional lines of male authority and, in Carol's experience at the salon, seems to have made appearance more important than other capacities she might have demonstrated as a hairdresser. Understanding these wider conventions of gendered authority and image might have helped Carol to question her own and others' construction of her as merely an accessory in the shop.

This is not to denigrate issues or personal style and its expressive importance to people. Rather, it is to open the question of whether or not it is possible to participate in the conventions of style without, at the same time, losing sight of how these conventions define and regulate the understandings we, and others, have of ourselves. In our view, this is a significant issue for both women and men. Working with and on student experience would therefore mean challenging Carol to locate her experience at the salon in a broader context. Carol, in other words, is not alone. Connecting her experience with that of others can reveal points of difference and similarity in how questions of appearance are regulated across a variety of worksites. How are claims made differently on men and women? What conventions of "image" operate at an office, a retail store, a garage, a radio station?

Teaching Note

This discussion of Carol's workplace experience, as with similar discussions throughout this chapter, is necessarily selective. Doing justice to the full complexity and richness of such experiences, as well as to their further embeddedness within relations of family, schooling, and personal history, is beyond the scope of our intentions here. What we wish to highlight are some of the issues that might be raised in relation both to the student workplace stories we were told and to questions of social relations at work.

Social conventions at the workplace are sets of practices that new workers must learn. Nevertheless, because this learning sometimes means a struggle over preferred ways of doing things, it is necessary to contextualize forms of resistance as well as compliance. Nicole, for example, in the following interview segment, shows how she resists workplace conventions concerning the wearing of uniforms in the drugstore where she works:

Like, one day my boss commented on my pants because the ankles were too tight. That wasn't the way the uniform was supposed to look. And I said, "Oh, okay," and he goes, "Can you fix them?" And I said, "Yeah, probably," right? And so I just left them. . . . I wasn't really sure whether he meant it or not actually, but . . . it's been, like, a month and a half and he hasn't said anything about it. So I think he was just kind of testing me to see if I was like a little worm or something, jump up at what he says. Because I think he respects people that can stand up to him.

Like Jennifer's response to her daycare center supervisor (see above), Nicole's way of dealing with the constraints on her wearing of the uniform can be both limited and limiting. Nicole undermines the effectiveness of her resistance to workplace conventions by privatizing the encounter with her boss and by locating it psychologically as a test of personality. The confusion of not really knowing what's going on further adds to the fragility of her resistance. This is understandable in light of the contradictory demands made on workers, like Nicole, to be at once adaptable but also prepared to stand up for themselves. In the final analysis, however, Nicole's way of handling her boss's intervention only perpetuates and reproduces the very lines of authority she is seeking to contest.

In a variety of class discussions, Nicole constantly returned to the theme of her personal resistance to what she viewed as petty and arbitrary uses of authority. This way of taking up issues of authority relations is common in discussions of work experience. However, at times such conversation can suppress a consideration of the notion of convention and its powerful effects in the workplace. Thus, additional questions that might be pursued in the wake of Nicole's story include: Why are employees required to wear uniforms? Who designs what the uniform looks like and why? Who decides what style of wearing a uniform is appropriate and inappropriate?

Theme 2: Showing and Taking Initiative

> Like, before, when I worked at the daycare center, I'd just get up in the morning and say, "I don't feel very well," so I wouldn't go. But at the elementary school I'm working at now, I'll stay up till, like, five in the morning reading or watching TV and I'll still get up in the morning and go. Like, I've never missed a day.
>
> (Leslie)

Initiative is often thought of in individual terms. Showing enterprise, interest, and an ability to make decisions about how to do one's own work are taken as personal characteristics that workers either possess or do not possess on entering the workplace. Workers, it is often said, lack interest in their work and are unwilling to take risks. Here, however, we take the approach that initiative, like competence and skill, is not simply a matter of personality, but also a capacity organized through the social relations of work. For Leslie, for example, as she recalls above, working at the school provided a sense of enthusiasm and responsibility that working at the daycare did not. How, then, do such differences get established? How does the opportunity to demonstrate interest and initiative get either expanded or diminished?

To begin to answer such questions, we need to make a distinction between "showing" initiative and "taking" initiative. This is a matter of some importance for students as they struggle to establish their credibility as workers in a new work environment. Showing initiative refers to the ability to demonstrate that you can do what the job entails, work independently, and express an interest in what you are doing. Taking initiative refers to the creativity and agency involved in seeing where changes can, or need to, be made in the way things are conventionally done at the workplace. Both aspects can be difficult for students, as they are generally for workers new to the job. Taking initiative, especially if it is seen to compromise one's recognition as a competent worker, can be threatening. There is also the very real fear, as many students have expressed it, of making mistakes, particularly when high demands are made on individual performance.

Opportunities to show initiative can be diminished in situations in which students' participation in work processes is limited to a small range of routine tasks and activities. Jim's work, for example, as a mechanic at a garage consisted mainly, as he explained it, of "changing tires and batteries." Although Jim was both capable of and interested in doing more, his participation on the job did not allow this to emerge. Neither was *showing* initiative in accelerating the pace of his work, in handling the job on his own, and in occupying his spare time by observing other mechanics particularly recognized or valued. Eventually frustrated by the routine nature of the work, Jim took the initiative to ask his supervisor for something more challenging to do, like brakes. Not only was his request only briefly accommodated, but it also brought him into direct conflict with the supervisory assistant who was quite content to keep Jim on tires, as this was normally the assistant's job. Clearly, Jim's age and lack of status on the job intersected with lines of authority and convention in ways that reduced his ability to act effectively on his sense of initiative. When we add to this the fact that it was late fall and tire changes were in demand, and that Jim's status as an unlicensed mechanic prevented him from doing more sophisticated repair work, we can see how the opportunities to take initiative (for example, to define new and challenging things to do) are shaped and regulated within the wider organization of work at the garage.

Derek's work at an electrical supplies manufacturing plant raises other issues around initiative that teachers may wish to take up with students. Derek, for example, not only met but excelled at his employer's expectations of competence and productivity on the job. His ability to work rapidly and accurately through assigned tasks was a source of personal pleasure and accomplishment. Nevertheless, this showing of initiative was met with suspicion by veteran workers at the plant who, at the time, were facing the possibility of job layoffs. As Derek recalls, in connection with his pace of work: "I just kept working and working, right. I stayed at my own pace, and then, I slowed down a bit, but I kept up more than I should . . . just a bit more, you know. Just to keep them pleased, that I'm really trying my best, right."

Derek's showing of initiative (keeping up "more than he should") takes place on ambiguous grounds—grounds of which he is only partially aware. It is here that the divergent interests of union and management compete for his sense of allegiance and responsibility, and where he must reconcile his own expectations of competence with those already established in the workplace. Working *with* and *on* experience so as to help make such interests visible is fundamental to the kind of pedagogical project we are suggesting here. Helping students see alternatives, for example, to the belief that initiative is a wholly personal and individual phenomenon is integral to this project.

Theme 3: Authority at Work

> . . . I spent the whole afternoon cutting squares of fabric. I didn't come into contact with the kids at all. . . . It kind of made me mad because I'm not there to play slave to her. . . . That's what it felt like to me and I didn't know what to say so I didn't say anything. . . . She didn't even ask me, "Would you mind?" She was like, "Well, you can just do it." Shut up and do it, I dunno. . . . Like I'm not capable of working with the children or something. . . . She didn't seem to treat me like she treated anybody else, like she wouldn't have asked anybody else to cut them.
>
> (Nicole at a daycare center)

Breaking the silence that confrontations with authority in the workplace can bring into play is a difficult and demanding process. Authority relations at work, like elsewhere, play on the affective investments we make in our sense of ourselves as capable and creative participants in the workplace. Contradicting the grounds of these investments can produce feelings of anger, exclusion, and being taken advantage of, which can compromise our ability both to fit in and to see what fitting in entails.

As Nicole recalls above, she experienced the encounter with her supervisor as an abuse of authority that undermined her sense of self and prevented her from responding in any way other than passively. Nicole's reaction is, in many ways, legitimate; her supervisor failed to address her with respect, she did not contextualize the task of cutting squares in a way that made it seem meaningful to her, and she left Nicole feeling inferior to other teachers at the center as well as to the main work of caring for children. This sense of legitimate anger is important. A pedagogy that begins by valuing student experience needs to take this into account as a viable place to start in discussing relations of authority in the workplace. Challenging Nicole to think further about her experience does not mean "undoing" the anger by accounting for it in purely rational terms. The task of altering authority relations in the workplace does not, after all, rest with workers, like Nicole, alone. Rather, it requires shifting the grounds of the anger so as to make it more conducive to the possibility of effecting change in the workplace and of claiming a sense of agency in the determination of one's working life. How, then, can a perspective based on understanding social relations at work assist students like Nicole to deal more productively with confrontations with authority?

Students need to have opportunities to speak of their problems with authority in the workplace. These include not only formal relations of authority between workers and bosses but also informal relations between new workers, for example, and more senior and 'expert' workers. It is through the exchange of such stories that problems with authority can be contextualized not as individual matters to be handled privately, but as issues that are socially organized and historically constituted. Within this view, authority is not something possessed by individuals or the positions they hold, but rather, a relationship produced and reproduced through the daily activities of doing work. Authority, in other words, is a relationship that is socially constructed; as such, it is open to question and, potentially, to being constructed differently.

Being aware of the ways in which authority is socially produced might help students like Nicole avoid explanations such as "That's just the way she [the supervisor] is" and "There's nothing I can do about it." In Nicole's case at the daycare center, lines of authority are established through the specific relations of professional certification, expertise, age, seniority, and experience, that working with preschool children entails. It is these organizational features of the workplace that may need addressing when conflicts over authority arise, rather than simply the personality of the supervisor in question.

Nicole, like many students, commented that she didn't know what to say to her supervisor, and could therefore only respond with silence. Being aware of how her relationship with her supervisor is organized through social relations at the center might give Nicole different grounds on which to formulate a response. By addressing, for example, the issue of how tasks at the daycare center are allocated (including unchallenging but necessary tasks like preparing materials for teaching) and how they connect to other tasks that together form the work of the center, Nicole might find that she is not considered the "slave" that she feels her supervisor judges her to be. This does not mean emphathizing with the supervisor's position, and therefore condoning it, but it does mean taking charge of one's anger differently and realizing that authority relations are not simply matters of personality or arbitrary expressions of power.

Teaching Note

Acquiescence to authority and the silencing it can produce are particularly damaging in cases where sexual and economic exploitation may be at issue. Students who suffer harassment on the job and feel isolated, silenced, and personally at fault especially need alternate ways of conceptualizing, and acting upon, the relations of power that gendered workplace practices bring into play. Harassment is not a random occurrence; it is neither a matter of bad luck nor is it disconnected from wider social and cultural conventions of gender. In this sense, being able to act is not only a question of seeing the organization of authority relations in the workplace, but also of giving oneself permission to be angry, that is, creating the conditions that enable claiming responsibility for oneself. This is not always easy to do and often requires the help of teachers, friends, parents, and support agencies.

Theme 4: Taking up an Identity

Every single day I've got something different to do. . . . And the teacher, she really depends on me. . . . She trusts me, like, she can leave the class, and . . . I can control the class now.

(Leslie at an elementary school)

Well, at first you know, . . . I felt so young and I should be in school or something. But then after a while, after I got to know everybody, it was okay, like, you know, I was just another worker here.

(Tony at a furniture design shop)

Both Leslie and Tony, each in their own way, have come to feel a part of workplace relations and routines. For Leslie, the satisfaction of taking responsibility for her work and the validation she receives from others produces a sense of self-affirmation that supports her understanding of herself as a future teacher. For Tony, overcoming the limitations of age and the feeling of being accepted on his own terms support the sense of belonging he values as part of his work learning to be a cabinetmaker. For Leslie, especially, working at the elementary school has opened up possibilities for defining a work identity within which she can feel a sense of accomplishment and confidence.

Such moments of affirmation can be important resources for exploring how work identities get shaped through the social relations of work. How does Leslie, for example, come to take up a position at the school that allows her to recognize herself as a future teacher? What helps to establish this recognition? How does she come to "feel like" a teacher, and what helps others to acknowledge her as such?

In the first example, Leslie was encouraged by her supervising teacher to exercise autonomy during both the preparation for and actual teaching of the class. She was also informed of the particular philosophies and techniques of education that were part of her supervisor's teaching practice at the school. Knowing not only what to do and how to do it, but also how to think and talk about it, are then important aspects of demonstrating autonomy. Exercising autonomy, however, involves something more. It also requires being able to take risks even in the knowledge that mistakes might be made. Feeling justified in taking risks makes for an expanded sense of self-confidence and agency in the workplace. In feeling capable of controlling the class, Leslie is confirmed in her ability and desired to work with children. What this implies is that, under different circumstances and working conditions, Leslie might not have felt affirmed as a future teacher. That is, if students, as workers, do not feel affirmed in the same way as Leslie, it is not simply because they themselves are at fault. Rather, certain patterns of social relations at work can either enhance or limit possibilities for taking up particular work identities. Feelings of affirmation, in other words, like feelings of exclusion, are produced through the ways in which capacities are selectively valued and taken up in the workplace.

This sense of accomplishment is, however, not without ambiguity. Feeling a part of existing workplace practices and identities, while affirming, can also preclude other ways of thinking about what, for example, it means to be a teacher, cabinetmaker, hairdresser, mechanic, or indeed, just another worker. Being a teacher is not just an individual matter of confirmation and competence; neither does it exist in a social vacuum. Existing perceptions of teaching, like perceptions of working in other occupations, are situated within wider social, cultural, and historical contexts. Many of these perceptions reproduce taken-for-granted ideas about what teaching, and being a teacher, are about. What else is at stake when, for example, as a part of her work identity, Leslie says she feels comfortable "controlling" the class? Or when Tony refers to himself as "just another worker?" These are concerns about work identities and public perceptions of what groups of people as workers must be like, that teachers might want to address with their students. Feeling a part of things is an obvious and important goal for student workers who are new to the job. However, it is also important to recognize that feeling integrated can leave unquestioned what such integration might entail.

SECTION TWO: STUDENT STORIES AND DISCUSSION QUESTIONS

Suggestions for Case Discussion

The following cases are provided to help orient discussion around the themes of convention, initiative, authority, and identity addressed in

Section One above. While the overall intention is to help students understand how work identities and problems at work are socially produced, and how alternatives may be envisaged, this is not to presume that right answers exist. Rather, the stories can serve as catalysts for students to exchange similar or contradictory experiences they may have had during their own work placements. In many cases, providing the opportunity to voice difficulties, and staying with the contradictions they generate, is likely to be more important than working toward resolutions. While discussion questions are suggested at the end of each story, additional issues have been raised in Section One. Teachers may wish to refer back to this section for further resources or clarification.

Working with these stories need not be limited to large group discussion. Different issues from each story could be taken up by smaller groups and then exchanged; role-plays between characters in a given story could be enacted; individual or group responses could be done in writing or recorded on tape; different stories can be developed and added. Finally, the focus of the stories is two-fold: on both particular places of work and issues of social relations. Learning to move across workplace boundaries and to recognize points of similarity and difference in the ways things are done and valued is a major aspect of working with experience and of envisaging collective strategies for change.

At a Daycare Center

Working with children is something Sue has always enjoyed. She has had experience helping her mom, who provided childcare services at home, and she has done a lot of babysitting in her spare time after school. She thinks working as a daycare teacher is something she would like to do in future, and has considered staying in school to get her Early Childhood Education certificate.

After a few days at the daycare center where she is now working, however, Sue is having second thoughts. All of the other teachers are quite a lot older than Sue; they have little in common, and there never seems to be any time to talk. Yesterday, when she went to comfort a child who was crying, another teacher came up and took over, giving Sue the feeling that she was considered incapable of handling the problem on her own. This has happened on a number of occasions. Sue didn't feel it was her place to ask questions, so she didn't say anything about her frustrations either to her supervisor or to any of her co-workers. Often, she feels left alone to figure things out herself.

Sue enjoys the moments at the center when she can be on her own with the children and when, on occasion, she has responsibility for setting up for lunch or snack times. But there aren't enough moments like this. She often finds herself doing things at the center that keep her from spending time with the children. This afternoon, for example, her time was spent going through a pile of magazines looking for pictures the children might use later for art work. She feels that the supervisor wouldn't have asked anybody else to do this, and that she asked Sue just because she didn't want to do it herself. She feels left out of the real work at the center and, despite her desire to work with children, is starting to feel inadequate for the job. She is even beginning to think that daycare work isn't really what she wants to do after all.

Places to Start

How does Sue's experience in caring for children at home compare with her experience of childcare at the daycare center?

What prompted the other daycare teacher to intervene as Sue was comforting one of the children? Are there ways in which Sue could interpret this teacher's action differently?

Why didn't Sue feel it was her place to ask questions? If she did feel more comfortable, what kinds of questions might she ask?

How does Sue feel about being given the task of choosing pictures from magazines? Is this simply "a part of the job?"

Is the supervisor personally to blame for making it difficult for Sue to feel a part of the center?

At a Machine Shop

Howard wants to be a machinist. He's made machine shop his specialty over the last two years at school and he's hoping to get an apprenticeship as a machinist, like his brother, when he's finished. He likes working different kinds of machines and sees his co-op placement as a way of learning more and increasing his skills.

The machine shop Howard is working at now is a small business with only about five employees; as Howard describes it, everyone works at virtually all the tasks at the shop, including the owner and the manager. All the same, Howard's main job there, contrary to what he expected, is packing up and labelling customer orders for delivery. What Howard really wants to do is work on the lathe in order to get some experience at something new. Although the manager said he shouldn't be afraid to ask questions, Howard still didn't feel comfortable doing so. The one time he asked to be changed to working on the lathe, the manager told him that packing was more important at the moment and that he'd just have to wait. Howard felt that the packing work was a waste of his time and that he was placed there only because the company could save money by not having to pay someone else to do it. Ultimately, despite his desire to improve himself as a machinist, Howard had little opportunity to demonstrate either his competence or his initiative to his employer. Ironically, his knowledge and expertise were recognized by at least one co-worker who continuously sought Howard out for advice.

Howard's shop teacher felt this would be a good placement for him. Howard, he commented, had a bad temper on occassion and would benefit from a place where the work was clearly organized, manageable, and structured in a way that would encourage him to practice self-control.

Places to Start

What influenced Howard's ability to show initiative?

Should work-study students be considered the same as regular employees?

To what extent should a student on work-study be allowed to participate in defining the terms of his or her employment?

When students, like Howard, feel that their needs on the job are constantly repressed, what should they do? What should teachers do?

Even if there was a prior agreement between Howard, his employer, and his teacher about what Howard would be doing on the job, does the employer have the right to ignore it if he needs Howard to do something different because the situation at work has changed?

At a Fast-Food Counter

Maria works part time behind the counter at a fast-food restaurant. She needs the money to get her through the week and finds that the hours fit in well with her work at school. All the same, Maria has some reservations about her job that she has trouble sorting out.

When she was first hired, her boss told her that business was slower than expected and that he was having financial difficulties. Hiring someone like Maria, who was 18, would mean paying out wages that he couldn't really afford. After all, he explained, he could hire someone equally good who was only 14, and pay them less per hour. As a result, he decided to pay Maria at minimum wage for two days of the week, and below minimum wage for the remaining two days.

Maria feels this arrangement is inadequate but finds it, in some ways, a fair trade-off for the fact that her boss also does her favors in return, like paying her in cash, giving her occasional advances, and not deducting taxes. Her sympathy for her boss's financial circumstances and her fear of losing a job that she needs make her feel that it's inappropriate to ask questions or to confront him about her rate of pay. Besides, as she says of herself, she's a "terrible counter-girl" anyway. She has noticed another worker at the place who is younger than she is, has learned the job more quickly, and is altogether more competent at serving the customers. Maria speaks of herself as getting confused sometimes under pressure and recalls one occasion in which her boss had to come to the front to help her out. Because of this, Maria feels that in many ways she doesn't really deserve the extra pay.

Places to Start

What counts as loyalty on the job?

How does Maria's sense of loyalty to her boss affect her understanding of how she is paid?

How does Maria's understanding of herself as a poor worker affect her ability to think differently about her working conditions?

At a Radio Station

This is how Mike talks about one of his days working at a local radio station:

Today I successfully operated *all* of the many controls for "Newswave" and was very impressed with myself. The best part is TODAY ... 18,000 people heard my name and voice. Tomorrow I will be co-hosting for one hour (amazing!). In the morning I actually wrote two news stories for the program (and typed). My afternoon was spent with the Program Director, as we went to pick up equipment. My day was the best.

Mike really enjoys his job; it give him a feeling of accomplishment and belonging that he has rarely had before. Since starting at the station, he has learned to do a number of new things and has had opportunities to put what he already knows into practice. He has, for example, learned to edit, to work under the pressure of producing a program to deadline, and to cover "dead air time" on the show when something goes wrong. Although he has made some mistakes, he's been quick to correct them and feels confident about working on his own. He enjoys the support of his co-workers at the station, something that became clear when he eventually was allowed to host his own two-hour show. As he said, he had to choose and mix the right kind of music, and decide on the right amount of talking. Although he was worried about doing a good job, it turned out that he felt comfortable on the air after all, and the show was a big success. Not only did he get assistance from the other workers, but they all came up afterward and complimented him on the way the program had gone. Although there are slow times at the station when there isn't much to do, Mike doesn't mind this too much. In general, Mike feels good about himself and about the kind of work he's doing.

Places to Start

How does the way in which work is done at the radio station help Mike to feel that he fits in?

What kinds of things does Mike do that make him feel like a real radio announcer?

What are the features and relations of a workplace that help new workers like Mike to show and take initiative?

What kinds of things does he do that encourage others at the workplace to think of him as a real announcer?

At a Family Restaurant

Linda is waitressing part-time in a restaurant. She works hard, often putting in extra effort and hours. But this usually goes unacknowledged by the owner of the restaurant and his wife, Anne, both of whom Linda feels aren't really doing their fair share of work there.

Although she doesn't like to talk about it much, Linda is particularly disturbed and angry by the way the owner of the restaurant treats her and interferes with her work. She often catches him staring at her and making suggestive remarks about her appearance. As she says, "Every time I looked up, he was, like, making rude sounds, you know ... sort of all hands all the time ... and he'd say, 'Come here, I gotta tell you something.' And then he'd, you know, be really rude and do something in my ear, kiss me, and I just didn't like that."

If she tried to say she didn't like it, he would laugh it off or argue that she had asked for it anyway, given the provocative way she wore her uniform. Anne doesn't give Linda any support in this because she too is used to having her comments dismissed as "crazy" by him. Away from the restaurant, Linda refers to him as a "pervert," and feel that the only way out is to quit and apply for work at another restaurant.

Places to Start

Part of what counts as Linda's appearance is how she is said to be wearing her uniform. How do women workers, like Linda, reconcile the contradiction between needing to look good for the job, and at the same time running the risk of having their appearance called provocative?

Is it up to Linda to change her appearance?

Is Linda's experience an unusual or exceptional one? If not, how can you explain the prevalence of such experiences?

What options might be open to her other than quitting?

At a Residence for the Elderly

Theresa has been working as an assistant for some time now at a residence for elderly people who require nursing and psychiatric care. She was shocked at first by the peculiar ways the residents behaved at the home, by the smell of the place, and by the harsh way some of the nurses and doctors handled the patients, but has gradually become accustomed to it. Theresa's friend, Mike, thinks that working at a residence is easy and just a matter of commonsense. After all, he says, everybody has grandparents and there's nothing special about learning to relate to them; it's just a question of habit. Theresa throws her hands up in despair and tells him about some incidents that have happened recently at the residence.

Theresa was asked to take one of the patients downstairs one afternoon to watch a movie. This particular resident was known for her stubbornness about routines and group activities at the residence, but this time she protested even more loudly at being forced to move. She suddenly started screaming and refused to get into the elevator. Theresa wasn't sure what to do. She felt the resident was owed respect because of her age, but she also felt her outburst was excessive. She had also learned at school that nurses should always be supportive of patients. The other nurses, though, intervened and started yelling at the resident, saying she shouldn't be allowed to do that, the activity was for her own good, and Theresa should just get her into the elevator. Theresa felt uncertain, but complied.

Some time later, Theresa was with two other patients at the residence who spent their time each day fighting, hurling insults, and occasionally slapping and pinching each other. Because Theresa had become used to hearing the nurses' aides yell at the patients about things they shouldn't be doing, she decided she might as well do the same, and so resolved the situation by shouting at them to stop. This left her feeling uncomfortable and unsure as to whether she had done the right thing.

Theresa finds most of the nurses at the residence to be okay, but she has reservations about one nurse's authoritarian way of dealing with the patients. She feels Margaret is too quick to criticize patients for doing things that are really beyond their control, like wetting their pants. Rather than consoling them, Margaret tends to get rough and tells them they should know better. Nevertheless, Margaret's experience and expertise are respected at the residence, and Theresa feels obliged to agree with her way of doing things, even if they contradict her own sense of what is right.

Places to Start

How did Theresa learn what was expected of her as a nursing assistant at the residence?

In what ways do Theresa's expectations of caring for elderly patients differ from the expectations of the nurses at the residence? What accounts for these differences?

Who has the authority to decide how things are done at the residence and how patients are to be treated?

What consequences does "learning to yell" at the patients have for Theresa's understanding of herself as a future nurse?

Theresa doesn't agree with Margaret's way of handling the patients. Is there any way Theresa can show her disagreement without compromising her reputation at the residence?

7

Occupational Health and Safety: A Critical Look

The topic of occupational health and safety is a standard part of most work education programs in North America. In programs that include students' experiences in workplaces (like co-operative education and other forms of work-study), the emphasis is often defensive. That is, education about occupational health and safety is justified as a way of taking precautions in order to "assure the health, safety, and protection of students during the out-of-school component." Such a defensive posture usually means that there is a singular emphasis on providing information about safe work practices and safety equipment as well as worker protection within existing legislation.[1]

While such information is important, to limit teaching about occupational health and safety to the provision of safety tips and copies of government legislation is not enough. Health and safety should be more than the distribution of fact sheets or the presentation of safety issues through a video cassette. Indeed, once we begin to take a critical look at the topic of occupational health and safety, we can begin to see how it may operate as another window on the complex world of work.

There are at least four key themes that can focus a critical student inquiry into the topic of occupational health and safety. Each theme contains within it a number of important issues related to the central concerns of this book. The activities that make up this chapter are organized in relation to these four key themes.

THEME I: THE DEFINITION OF A HEALTH AND SAFETY PROBLEM

What is a health and safety problem? This is by no means a trivial issue. Someone, somewhere, at some time, has to identify a particular situation or condition and name it as an occupational health and safety problem. Within these activities students are asked to consider who does this naming and how it is done. The fact that the naming of a health and safety problem is a human decision implies that there may be disagreements over how and when such decisions are made. In our view, it is important for students to understand how and why such disagreements may arise and what may be done to resolve such disputes.

THEME II: THE ALLOCATION OF RESPONSIBILITY FOR SOLVING THE PROBLEM

Once a situation or condition has been defined as a health and safety problem, the question arises as to whose responsibility it is to correct the situation or solve the problem. As we have argued in other chapters (Chapter 4, Skills and Work Design), how a problem is defined (and by whom) has direct implications for the allocation of responsibility for correcting the situation or solving the problem. There are three common types of solutions to occupational health and safety problems, each with its own preferred locus of responsibility. These are technical solutions (e.g., engineered controls like the redesign of equipment or processes, the substitution of materials), administrative solutions (e.g., better training, job rotation, longer rest periods), and personal solutions (e.g., wearing protective equipment, using proper methods for lifting). Note that each of these types of solutions implies differing degrees of responsibility among workers, management, and technical experts. As future workers, students would benefit by being aware of the implications of how health and safety problems are defined, both in terms of the solutions that are consequently seen as plausible and the resulting actions that they themselves might be held responsible for.

THEME III: OCCUPATIONAL HEALTH AND SAFETY AND THE SOCIAL CONTEXT OF WORK

Individual workers or groups of workers enter into production processes in ways that have particular health and safety implications. How people do their work is indeed a complex process determined by myriad physical and social factors. Just alerting people to potential hazards at work does not ensure that they will alter their everyday work routines or customary work practices. Students ought to come to some understanding of the various relationships in the workplace that affect how people interpret and act on health and safety information. In order to understand why, for instance, workers sometimes ignore health and safety precautions or why supervisors sometimes ignore health and safety violations, it may be important to consider how activities in the workplace are influenced by particular forms of wage-labor exchange, authority relations, and gender relations.

THEME IV: COLLECTIVE RESPONSIBILITY FOR HEALTH AND SAFETY

Discussions of occupational health and safety should not only be informed by issues of workers' rights but also by the notion of workers' responsibilities. It is important to stress not only the importance of individual responsibility, but the matter of collective responsibility as well. Also important is the necessity at times for workers to act jointly to protect themselves and improve the quality of their own working environment. In order to provide students with a sense of how this might be possible, it is important that they be given a chance to pursue questions such as: Have workers been able to initiate significant changes in their work environment that have created a safer and healthier workplace? If so, how have they organized themselves and used information, expertise, and the law to see that such changes were carried out? What factors militate against worker-initiated struggles for change?

Teaching Note

The activities in this chapter are based on the assumption that information concerning basic workplace health and safety precautions and workers' rights to a safe workplace have been provided to students. Information and teaching suggestions pertaining to these topics are widely available and we have chosen not to duplicate them here. We wish to stress, however, that this decision in no way minimizes the importance of such activities.

This chapter is organized as follows.

- Theme I: The definition of a health and safety problem
  Activity One: Health hazards at work: sources and solutions
  Activity Two: A health and safety audit of your workplace
- Theme II: Who is responsible for solving problems?
  Activity Three: Contrasting messages about health and safety
- Theme III: Occupational health and safety and the social context of work
  Activity Four: Why some workers ignore health and safety
  Activity Five: A refusal to work role play

• Theme IV: Collective responsibility for health and safety
  Activity Six: A case study of collective action

THEME I: THE DEFINITION OF A HEALTH AND SAFETY PROBLEM

Activity One: Health Hazards at Work—Sources and Solutions

The purpose of this activity is to have students consider the problems associated with answering the question: What is a health and safety problem? This consideration is facilitated by having students identify a range of work situations and conditions that they consider potential health and safety problems and then suggest how such situations might be alleviated or prevented. This is a deceptively simple activity with a number of complex teaching issues to reflect on. A suggested sequence is presented interspersed with a number of teaching notes.

What to Do in the Classroom

Based on their experiences in either part-time work or work placements associated with programs like cooperative education, ask students to list possible causes of accidents, injury, or illness they have observed while working. Keep a temporary record of the suggested possibilities.

Teaching Note

One of the difficult problems in teaching about health and safety is that some students can become overwhelmed by the number of workplace hazards that can be identified. This can lead to despair and passivity. When asked what one should do to prevent accident, injury, or illness, someone may very well call out, "Don't work!" A critical pedagogy of work education must try to minimize inquiry that does nothing other than reinforce feelings of resignation, hopelessness, and powerlessness in the face of difficult and undesirable situations. That is why the material in this chapter goes beyond the identification of problems and the limited possibilities of protective personal action. We believe it is also important for students to grasp how more comprehensive solutions might be defined and to recognize when it might be necessary for workers to take collective responsibility for creating a safe workplace. Teachers considering this chapter should thus allow enough time when planning lessons for these issues to be discussed

Using this list, ask students to generate suggestions that would help eliminate these problems. Keep a temporary record of these suggestions.
Ask students to consider their lists of problems and solutions, indicating which items assume that the basic problem is one of personal carelessness (the solution to which is a greater sense of personal re-

sponsibility for oneself) and which items indicate problems that individuals would have a hard time remedying or avoiding. If there is an imbalance between these categories, note this and have the class consider what might account for the imbalance.

Teaching Note

It is important to work on such student-generated lists, calling attention to the framework through which our everyday understanding of health and safety issues are generated. Consider the following list of workplace dangers produced by an eleventh-grade class in a ten-minute discussion:

falling downstairs	*clumsiness*
inhaling chemicals	*dangerous machines*
cuts and amputation	*horseplay*
mental illness	*boredom*
carelessness	*speeding up*
watching the clock	*anger*
frustration	*machinery abuse*
lack of maintenance	*ignoring supervisors*
fooling around	*smoking dope*
too much pressure	*lack of instruction*
lack of interest	*physical exhaustion*
poor air	*dirty environment*
not having proper equipment	*dust*
working if they need me but I don't feel well	*carbon monoxide*

The majority of items on this list reflect the idea that most workplace hazards are a result of individual thoughtlessness or carelessness. The prevalence of this mode of thinking about health and safety is not surprising. That we should take personal responsibility for our own health and safety is a dominant and recurrent message in society. This dominant mode of thought is further illustrated in the list of suggestions this class generated for resolving some of these problems:

always wear safety equipment	*close the plant down*
clean yourself up	*be wide awake*
keep work area clean	*safety inspections*
care about yourself	*care about others*

beware of causes of accidents   *follow rules*

proper procedures   *have a union*

Again, note here the dominance of suggestions that presume individual respon-sibility as the solution. This represents a form of "imbalance" referred to above. Making the framework that generates this imbalance evident, and discussing what keeps us thinking predominantly along these lines are important teaching tasks within this activity. What is to be stressed is not, of course, that it is wrong to take responsibility for your own safety, but rather that solutions that emphasize individual behaviors may only be one of a number of possible alternatives.

Compare the students' lists of workplace hazards with a standard list offered by government, employer, or union organizations distributing information on workplace safety. What hazards do the students mention that official pamphlets do not? What hazards do the pamphlets mention that students do not? Discuss with the class what they notice about this.

Teaching Note

We provide here a comparison of the students' lists with a fairly standard categorization scheme of workplace hazards. (Note: an asterisk indicates that the hazard was identified by students.)

hazardous atmosphere*   *electrical hazards*

construction hazards   *dangerous machinery**

vibration   *welding hazards*

falls*   *noise*

heat stress   *cold stress*

manual lifting   *biological hazards*

toxic substances   *reproductive hazards*

chemicals*   *dusts and fibers**

lighting   *stress*

air quality   *radiation*

fatigue*   *excessive sitting*

excessive standing

Note that students did not identify (that is, did not in their experience define as hazardous) such things as vibration, noise, extremes of temperature, lighting, air quality, and excessive sitting or standing. It may be that these things are seen as "just part of the job," it may be that they don't seem to pose serious health risks, or perhaps students never before thought of such issues as health issues. Also interesting is the emphasis students put on behavior. Their list includes such things as: clumsiness, horseplay, carelessness, anger, fooling around, and smoking dope. Although "bad behavior" is not listed in the occupational health and safety literature as being a major source of health and safety problems (despite some employer claims of rampant substance abuse in workplaces), students seem to have bought into the argument that workers themselves are largely responsible for accidents on the job.

Reexamine student suggestions for eliminating hazards. What kinds of solutions are offered? See if the class can classify which suggestions require changes in worker behavior, changes in the organization of work, and engineering changes as to how the work is actually accomplished.

Teaching Note

Note the same sense of individual responsibility is evident in the students' proposed solutions to health and safety problems. With the exception of recommendations to close the plant, have a union, and require safety inspections, solutions to problems amount to being careful and following the rules: "Know-how on the job—you've got it, use it." Notably missing from the list are engineered controls that deal with health and safety hazards at the source. To focus attention on the importance of engineered or administrative solutions, however, requires going back to the problem of defining hazards and expanding students' understanding of what constitutes a health risk.

Manual lifting provides a good example to make this point. Lifting is the cause of many back problems, which are themselves a major category of occupational injury. When back injury is defined as an individual problem, it is the worker who is responsible for making sure that she or he lifts properly to avoid injury. The employer may train workers in proper lifting procedure, or hang up some posters with instructions and diagrams. When the problem is defined in terms of a production process that requires dangerous lifting, the solution is to design material handling systems that eliminate the hazard at the source. With this example in mind, the class can return to its list of sources and try to generate some engineered or administrative solutions to health and safety hazards at work.

Activity Two: A Health and Safety Audit of Your Workplace

A workplace health and safety audit is a good way of expanding students' understanding of the range of possible hazards that might exist in a workplace.

What to Do in the Classroom

Explain to students that the purpose of a health and safety audit is to identify possible workplace dangers that could cause accidents, illness, or injury. With the cooperation of their supervisor in their workplace, ask students to use the accompanying checklist of conditions and to write a report indicating any potential health and safety problems that might be investigated in their immediate work environment. Ask students to share their reports with their workplace supervisor and at least one employee and include in their report how these individuals view any problems the student thinks he or she has identified. If there are differences of opinion as to whether or not a student has identified a problem, have the class consider what might account for this difference.

Additionally, an in-class discussion based on the audit can lead to a consideration of why some workplaces are more involved than others in health and safety issues. Comparisons can be made between factories and offices, construction sites and food service industries, large and small organizations, unionized and non-union workplaces. The effectiveness of different strategies for dealing with workplace hazards can be addressed. Circumstances that lead to legislation supporting worker participation in and initiation of programs for improving working conditions can also be explored.

The following is a suggested format and list of questions through which the audit may be conducted. This is offered only as a suggestion. Preferably, students should participate in generating a manageable set of questions to guide their observations at their workplaces.

1. Work context

   Where do you work? What type of organization is it? How many full-time employees work in this organization? What kinds of goods/services do they produce/supply? What kind of area do you generally work in (e.g., office, kitchen, shop floor, construction site, etc.)?

2. Health and safety information

   Does the organization have a joint health and safety committee? Where are the names of members posted? Who on this committee represents workers? What health and safety information is posted in the workplace? Is there a written and signed copy of the workplace health and safety policy that you are aware of? Is there an emergency procedure that you are aware of? Is the procedure written down? Did anyone explain the emergency procedure to you before you asked about it? Have you had an emergency drill? What are you supposed to do if you see a hazard in the workplace? Whom do you tell if you get hurt and what is his or her responsibility in the workplace? Do you know where the first-aid supplies are kept?

3. Health and safety features in use

   Can you identify any engineered controls of potential workplace hazards (e.g., enclosures, ventilation, material handling systems, appropriately designed workbenches, desks, chairs, stools, etc.)?

Can you identify any administrative controls of potential workplace hazards (e.g., job rotation, rest periods, lockers and showers, written work procedures, labelling and safe handling instructions)?

Can you identify personal protective equipment in use (e.g., respirators, coveralls, goggles, gloves, ear plugs, etc.)? Were these pointed out to you?

4. Possible workplace hazards

As you walk around your workplace, look carefully at all the machines, tools, aisles, and work processes. Note if any of the conditions listed below exist.[2] Such conditions represent potential hazards.

Teaching Note

It will be important to review with the class why certain of the following categories represent health and safety risks. Some students may not consider some items as serious hazards. In this case, they should be urged to investigate if other personnel in the workplace feel the same way or not. Such students should also be challenged to explain why organizations promoting occupational health and safety want to call such items to workers' attention.

Air quality. Are surfaces covered with dust, film, or corrosion? Are there visible clouds of fumes coming from equipment or the ventilation system? Is the air thick with particles or dust? Are there strong odors in the workplace? Do workers experience any of the following problems: eyes burning or watering; sore throat or irritation of the nasal cavity; coughing or breathing difficulties; rashes or other skin problems; headaches, dizziness, nausea; numbness; changes in health, behavior or moods; persistent symptoms of ill health?

Machinery. Do the machines in your workplace have safety guards? Are there any exposed moving parts that could catch clothes, hair? Are the starting and stopping devices within reach of the operator? Is there danger of machinery starting by itself? Can switches be secured in position during repairs? How often is machinery checked by maintenance workers? Repaired? Cleaned? Tuned up?

Equipment. Are power tools maintained? Do they have proper guards? Are you required to work with sharp objects? Are you required to work with heavy equipment? Does your personal equipment fit properly? Is it the right weight for you? How often are you required to wear personal safety equipment? Are load capacities clearly marked on hoists and cranes? Is emergency equipment available and properly maintained?

Substances. Can you identify the materials you work with? Do you know which substances are hazardous? Are hazardous substances like chemicals and biological agents clearly labeled? Have you been trained to read these labels? Have you been trained in procedures for safe handling, storage, and disposal of these hazardous materials?

Floors. What kinds of floor surfaces do you work on? Are the floors and aisles cluttered? Slippery? Wet? Do you have clear access to exits in case of emergency? Are exits clearly marked?

Wiring. Is there exposed wiring? Does any wiring run across the aisles? Is it grounded, secured, insulated? Are any electrical outlets overloaded?

Noise and vibration. Can you hear people when they talk in a normal tone of voice? Can you hear a shouted warning? Is there a heavy vibration while you are using any of the machines or equipment?

Lighting. Is there enough light to see to work properly? Do you have to strain your eyes while working? Is the lighting good in places where you use dangerous equipment?

Radiation. Do you work near x-rays, VDTs, or CRTs? Have the dangers of radiation been explained to you? What kinds of precautions or procedures are in place to prevent excessive exposure to radiation?

Temperature. Is your workplace too hot or too cold to work in properly? Are there sudden changes in temperature between different areas of your workplace?

Excessive sitting or standing. Are you required to spend long periods of time in the same position? Is your work station well designed and suitable for the work being done? Are you provided with periods of time to sit down or walk around?

Job atmosphere. Do you feel over-supervised or harassed on the job? Are you required to work too quickly? Is your job monotonous? Is there evidence of racism or sexual discrimination at your workplace? Does the work environment promote positive social relationships?

THEME II: THE ALLOCATION OF RESPONSIBILITY FOR SOLVING THE PROBLEM

Activity Three: Contrasting Messages about Health and Safety

There are many government agencies, public interest research groups, labor unions, and business organizations producing information and resources for studying occupational health and safety issues. Yet the messages contained in these materials are not always consistent, and at times seem contradictory. Often the discrepancy has to do with the allocation of responsibility for workers' health and safety. Materials produced by business organizations and government agencies are based on an analysis that stresses individual responsibility. Materials produced by unions and public interest groups tend to stress government and corporate responsibility.

This activity requires that teachers locate materials on health and safety from more than one type of organization. For example, in Ontario the Workers' Compensation Board funds several groups that are involved in occupational health and safety education. One of these groups, the Industrial Accident Prevention Association (IAPA), is a federation of industry safety associations supported by employers. Another group, the Workers' Health and Safety Centre, is a labor-affiliated organization concerned primarily with the education of joint health and safety committee representatives. Materials would be required from both organizations.

What to Do in the Classroom

Ask students to consider the implicit messages embedded in these materials. What assumptions underlie the analysis and recommendations for improving workplace health and safety? Are the "facts" used to support the analyses in agreement? How does the interpretation of these facts differ? What notions of responsibility inform these materials? What arguments are made for and against the introduction of administrative controls? What are the arguments for and against the provision of protective equipment as a means of dealing with workplace hazards?

Teaching Note

This activity is a good follow up to Activity One. It builds on the notion that different health and safety solutions imply different foci of responsibility for eliminating problems. The activity works particularly well if one can locate information from different agencies that address the same potential danger (e.g., back injuries; see the last Teaching Note in Activity One above).

THEME III: OCCUPATIONAL HEALTH AND SAFETY AND THE SOCIAL CONTEXT OF WORK

Activity Four: Why Some Workers Seem to Ignore Health and Safety Precautions

Students are occasionally surprised to find co-workers not using prescribed protective equipment or circumventing safety procedures. They are often doubly surprised to find supervisors turning a blind eye to such infractions. The point of this activity is neither to encourage nor excuse such risk-taking on the part of students or regular employees. Rather, it is to provide a more conceptualized understanding of the relations of production that constrain the pursuit of a healthy and safe work environment. Such an understanding is a necessary prerequisite to formulating effective strategies for the control and correction of work-place hazards.

Employers do have an obvious interest in reducing the costs of accidents and occupational disease. However, issues of health and safety at work have a contradictory character as far as management is concerned. Certainly, chronic illness and disabling accidents reduce a company's level of productivity. For every day's work lost in Canada due to strikes and lockouts, six working days are lost through workplace accidents and disease. Companies therefore have a positive stake in making the workplace less hazardous. However, since improvements in facilities, modifications to work processes, and substitution of hazardous materials involve costs that might disadvantage a company's competitive position and/or reduce company profits, employers are often reluctant to act on the recognition of legitimate long-term health risks and favor instead the less costly strategy of controlling for immediate, short-term dangers.

Attempting to keeping down the cost of health and safety prevention means at times employers will opt for the least expensive strategy of providing workers with protective equipment and information while stressing that it is the workers' responsibility to use such information and equipment. As students may quickly find out, such responsibility is not always taken by all employees. Even when more expensive engineered controls are used to deal with hazards at the source, their effectiveness is at times reduced when workers circumvent their use (e.g., moving materials without using a hoist, not positioning a ventilation hood or safety guard). The question to explore in this activity is why this happens. Students may be able to get a sense of the reasons by looking at both the issue of control in the workplace and the social dynamics of "workfloor culture."

Control in the Workplace

In many organizations workers have very limited control over the nature and organization of the work they do. While they may, in some instances, be able to determine how they will accomplish some prescribed set of tasks and develop a style or technique for doing their work, the materials, tools, and equipment used, as well as the production process itself, are all controlled and organized by the employer. The exchange relations between an employee and an employer are also negotiated on the employer's terms and are aimed at maintaining high levels of production. Bonus, piecework, and modified piecework schemes intensify the pressure on workers to produce. Because protective equipment often hampers workers' movements, and safety procedures sometimes slow down the work process, some people may choose to work more quickly and comfortably by not using protective equipment and ignoring safety procedures. Although the costs of accidents and injuries are of concern to management, front-line supervisors charged with "getting production out" or "keeping things moving" may at times be willing to tolerate safety infractions in order to maintain productivity and avoid "hassling" workers. Under such circumstances, workers are forced to choose between a long-term interest in protecting health and safety and a more immediate pressure to "make production" and/or "earn bonus."

Workfloor Culture

In response to this kind of forced choice, often in conjunction with the realization that one potential consequence of raising health and safety issues is the elimination of jobs which could result from more stringent workplace regulation, a workplace culture may develop that valorizes risk-taking and denigrates health and safety concerns. Practices that are risky may become incorporated into the working knowledge (Chapter 3) of the workplace, thus taking on a desirable quality among workers.

To take what might be seen as an extreme and fanciful example, if all the drywallers on a construction site are wearing stilts rather than using ladders or scaffolding because it enables them to work faster and earn bonuses, skillful stilting becomes part of the working knowledge of the competent drywaller. The practice, though risky, is good for drywallers in that they make more money, and good for supervisors in that they make production. A ladder-using newcomer to such a site would be ridiculed not only for slow work and lack of demonstrable skill, but for being afraid and overly concerned about his or her well-being. Thus the culture of this workplace, developed in response to a particular structure of exchange relations, militates against the serious adoption of stilting as a health and safety issue.

Of course, not every workplace will have a culture that supports and encourages risky practices. Moreover, students may find a variety of workplace cultures in any given organization, some of which are more prone to the support of risk-taking than others; for example, young male workers are often more likely to exhibit a "macho" bravado in relation to workplace risks. The following suggestion, however, will allow students to consider the relevance of this issue in their own work environments.

What to Do in the Classsroom

Either in the context of the audit suggested in Activity Two above or as a separate effort, ask students to write down their impressions in regard to the following questions: Do your co-workers follow health and safety guidelines for doing their job? If not, why not?

Teaching Note

The suggestions offered as to how students might conduct a health and safety audit will give students an idea of how to judge whether health and safety guidelines are being violated. It is important to stress, however, that when possible, students should talk to the workers involved about the reasons for these infractions. If there are observable differences among workers as to who ignores health and safety practices, have students note what groups of people are more likely to engage in risks.

In small groups or together with the entire class, use the information provided by students to discuss the reasons that workers engage in risky behavior on the job. In order to move class discussion of these incidents beyond an attribution of individual irresponsibility and "craziness," ask students to consider as possible reasons for risk-taking both issues of work process organization and workplace culture. For example, students may be asked to consider if the method of pay encourages workers to "choose" between a good paycheck and safety at work. Does the organization of the work process encourage risk-taking? Are there alternative work methods that would be less hazardous? Is there social pressure among workers to do their jobs in a particular way with the result that health and safety issues are ignored? Do these pressures differ among workers of different ages, genders, ethnic or racial groups? If so, what do we have to know to understand this differentiation?

Activity Five: A Refusal to Work Role Play

Collective action is an effective way of dealing with hazardous working conditions. Workers who are organized and informed, who have investigated and researched a health and safety problem, and who know about existing standards and procedures are less likely to be ignored and better able to pressure employers into correcting workplace hazards. Still, there are times when the hazard is so immediate that a work refusal may be necessary.

In Ontario, the right to refuse unsafe work is found in Bill 70, the Occupational Health and Safety Act, and in Part IV of the Canada Labour Code. Both recognize the worker's right to refuse unsafe work without fear of reprisal. Those workers who are covered have the right to refuse work when there is reason to believe that the work is dangerous.[3] Moreover, an employer may not dismiss, suspend, discipline, threaten, or otherwise penalize a worker for exercising his or her rights under the law.

This activity asks students to engage in a role play of the possibility of work refusal. However, before enacting a work refusal, the class should discuss the kinds of situations in which such a course of action might be warranted. In a long-term effort to effect changes in the overall workplace environment, the coordinated actions of fellow workers, health and safety committee representatives, and/or government inspectors may be a more appropriate and effective strategy than a work refusal. In a short-term situation, when, for example, a worker is asked to work on a broken machine or without protective equipment, a work refusal might be the only option available.

What to Do in the Classroom

Have the class generate a list of situations drawn from their own workplace experiences in which a work refusal might be in order. Some examples are as follows:

- A student working at an automotive repair shop is told to "bag up" worn-out brake shoes. The student thinks the shoes contain asbestos and that dust might be harmful, although other workers bag shoes without masks.
- A student working in a restaurant is assigned to wash windows during slow periods. She must stand on the top step of a stepladder to reach the entire window, and she is afraid of heights.
- A student working at a VDT thinks she might be pregnant. She has read about exposure to radiation, although her boss tells her not to worry.
- A graphic arts student is told to clean silk screens in the basement of a studio. The label on the solvent says to use it only in well-ventilated area; the employer says to open the basement window.
- A student in upholstery is continually asked to move heavy furniture unassisted.
- A hairdressing student gets headaches every afternoon. She wonders about the chemicals she is working with.

Familiarize the class with the sequence of a work refusal by outlining the following steps on the board:

1. The worker tells his or her supervisor/employer that conditions are unsafe.
2. The supervisor investigates the situation with the worker and worker's representative present.
3. If after discussion there is agreement that the work is safe, the worker must go back to work.

    If after discussion there is agreement that the work is unsafe, the worker is reassigned.
4. If after discussion there is disagreement, the worker removes herself or himself to a safe place or is reassigned. The supervisor can assign the job to another worker, who must be told about the work refusal.

5. The worker or employer notifies a ministry inspector.
6. The inspector investigates the situation in the presence of the worker's supervisor and worker's representative.
7. If the work site is declared unsafe, it may be shut down until safe specifications are met.
8. If the work site is declared safe, the worker must return to the job.

Have students work together in small groups to develop reenactments of potential work refusal situations using the situations they have generated themselves or drawing on the list provided above. After each enactment have the rest of the class discuss the quality of the solution reached during the role play. Make sure they consider the relative balance of long- and short-term solutions that might be possible.

Teaching Note

As with all role plays, students must understand the purpose of the roles they take on. In addition, they must make preliminary decisions at the beginning of the enactment as to the point of view and personal interest that will be motivating their role play.

Each role play requires at least four characters: a worker, a supervisor, a worker's representative, and an inspector (additional characters can be added if desired, such as other workers). Students should understand who the worker's representative and inspector are as indicated in current health and safety legislation. In clarifying the options that might be enacted it will be useful to briefly discuss: Why is it important to have a representative present at certain points in the refusal process? Why it is necessary to have an inspector? Why can and would someone do work that someone else has refused to do?

After several groups have had the opportunity to role-play situations, consider the following questions with the class as a whole. Is refusing to work a viable option for the regular employees at your workplace? Is it an option for students in cooperative education and work experience programs? Are there structures and procedures in place to support a student's refusal to do what she or he considers to be unsafe work?

THEME IV: COLLECTIVE RESPONSIBILITY FOR HEALTH AND SAFETY

Activity Six: A Case Study of Collective Action

While there is a clear sequence of steps to be followed in an individual work refusal (see Activity 5), there is no mandated route for employees to follow in seeking to improve their shared working conditions. Case studies of collective action to eliminate workplace hazards and/or correct health and safety problems can, however, serve as examples from which to learn about strategies and approaches that have been effective in other settings and situations.

What to Do in the Classroom

The central activity suggested here is an in-depth discussion of an example of workers attempting to take collective action to improve the health and safety of their workplace.

Teaching Note

The difficulty in this activity is finding either first-hand, written, or visual accounts with enough information about the process of collective action, and not just statements about the achieved or failed improvements. In Ontario, current and back issues of At the Source, *published by the Workers Health and Safety Centre, is a good source of useful case study information. Alternatively, one could invite a representative from a local health and safety committee to speak to the class about a workplace hazard or problem that was dealt with effectively. Moreover, if access and scheduling allow, feature films like "Norma Rae," "Silkwood," or the Canadian National Film Board's "See No Evil" can be used as vehicles for class consideration.*

As a way of consolidating the study of case examples of collective efforts at workplace improvement, have students consider what conditions need to exist in order to generate and support successful collective action to improve workplace safety. After identifying these conditions, have them clarify what would have to be done in order to ensure these conditions exist.

Whatever approach to the case is taken, there are several points that should be emphasized:

- the importance of generating a broad base of support by involving as many co-workers as possible in the complaint and investigation

- the availability of outside resources and supports to help in the collection, organization, and use of information (these would include labor unions, federations of labor, committees or coalitions on occupational health and safety, and public interest research groups)

- the existence of standards and procedures regulating most conditions at work which government inspectors can investigate and enforce

NOTES

1. In Ontario, for example, this would include information about The Occupational Health and Safety Act; Workers Compensation; Workplace Hazardous Materials Information System (WHMIS).

2. This checklist is adapted from an IAPA (Industrial Accident Prevention Association) Co-op Student Workplacement Health and Safety Assignment (February 1988) and a Safety Checkpoints Audit in *A Worker's Guide to Health and Safety*, Windsor Occupational Safety and Health Council and Ontario Public Interest Research Group (Toronto: James Lorimer & Company, 1982).

3. Not all workers, however, are covered by legislation. In Ontario, for example, farm workers, domestic workers, teachers in elementary and secondary schools and universities, police officers and fire fighters, hospital workers, nursing home workers, ambulance and medical laboratory workers, inmates, patients of psychiatric institutions, and federal government workers *are not covered* by Bill 70. Federal government workers and workers involved in inter-provincial transportation and communications are covered (but not to the same degree) by the Canada Labour Code.

8

Time On and Off the Job: The Interrelation of Work, Desire, and Leisure

The way people work and how they understand and relate to others in the workplace is intimately and inextricably linked to other aspects of their lives. This chapter is intended to encourage students to explore and examine how one's working life is bound up with the pleasures, stresses, and commitments one finds off the job. What we want to emphasize is the importance of recognizing that how a person enters into the social, technical, and exchange relations at work will inevitably influence and be influenced by the desires and realities produced and confronted outside of paid employment.

As we pointed out in the introduction to this book, there is no such thing as "work in general." Work is always contextual and specific. Yet the context of work is not just the particular workplace where one makes a living. The context of work also includes one's particular family circumstances and the opportunities one has for enjoyable and fulfilling activities outside of the workplace. Such circumstances and opportunities are not completely independent of the realities of working life. We need to recognize therefore that the demands, challenges, and rewards of a job can influence both the quality of one's domestic life and the very possibility of leisure time.

Why is the interrelation between work, domestic life, and the desire for leisure time important for young workers to consider? What needs to be understood about this interrelation? These are complex questions that will not be fully answered by the activities in this chapter. Yet these questions cannot and should not be avoided. As a basis for developing the activities suggested below, we have chosen to emphasize two specific reasons why the work, leisure, and domestic interrelation is important for students to consider, specifying issues that might be stressed in each case.

UNDERSTANDING OTHERS' VIEWS OF THEIR JOBS

Our first reason for suggesting the importance of this theme is based on our premise that a critical pedagogy of work education must be attentive to both working on and with experience (see Introduction). What is at stake here in relation to this premise is the need to help students work *with* their experience, helping them make connections between their own comprehension of realities of working life and the understandings of others. The young worker often encounters a range of views about work from older workers. These views may be encouraging or confusing, often depending on whether they are congruent or in conflict with the younger person's own orientation toward her or his job. In order to learn from the experiences of others, one must be open to hearing what people are saying about the importance of work in their lives. But furthermore, to understand these views—to comprehend how they are formed—one must consider not only the specifics of how work is shaped within a work environment (see the chapters on working knowledge, and skills and work design) but also the interrelation of work with other aspects of one's life.

When people are asked about the part work plays in their lives, that is, its personal significance for them, responses range from the very expressive (e.g., "Work is of central importance to my personal development and life fulfillment") to the purely instrumental (e.g., "Work is a tiresome necessity for acquiring the resources I and my family need for survival") with combinations and variations in between. While an instrumental orientation to work might be most common and widespread in modern capitalist economies, it is by no means universal; neither is it uniformly distributed through the working population. However, the recognition of such variation should not hide the fact that there are systematic social realities that influence how people view their work. These realities are illustrated by consistencies expressed when such views are compared across class, age, and gender distinctions. Examples of differences organized within such distinctions are given in the following assertions commonly found in research on job satisfaction as well as in descriptive accounts of the significance of work in peoples lives.

• Those in high-status, high-paying jobs tend to expect intrinsic satisfactions from their work while those in low-status, low-paying jobs do not.

• Many young people desire meaningful work but find themselves forced to abandon this hope after a short time or (if they are lucky) are told they have to wait patiently for job advancement.

• Women often find the world of paid employment a satisfying place compared to the world of domestic labor although those who cannot afford domestic help often find themselves working a "double day."

What is to be stressed then is that personal statements about the significance of work in people's lives are rarely just idiosyncratic. If we are to understand why there are similarities and differences between our own views and those of others, it is essential that we are able to consider how these connections are rooted in our different positions in the organization of social relations in our society.

FACING THE FUNDAMENTAL TRADE-OFF

The second reason for the theme of this chapter is related to another central premise of a critical pedagogy of work education; rather than adapting to existing realities as if there were no other options, education should serve the purpose of enabling people to expand the range of possibilities in their lives. Most people make a living by exchanging their time and labor power for pay and whatever intrinsic satisfactions a particular job may bring. Despite promises of interesting and challenging jobs as advanced technology is introduced into the economy (see Chapter 13, "Future Work," for suggestions on how to critically examine such assertions), for many workers the actual substance of their work—what they do day in and day out—is of no particular significance in their lives. This of course is not to say that their work is unimportant. Indeed, financial security, identity, friendship, and sense of community are often directly linked to having a job. However, the actual work of most people provides very little in the way of opportunity for personal development and fulfillment. Hence, it comes to be viewed as only a means to enjoyment of life outside work.

If the opportunities for meaningful work and good pay are restricted, more and more workers will find themselves in a position of having to consider how to balance a viable trade-off between what they have to do at work and what they want to do off the job. What might a critical pedagogy of work education concern itself with in the face of the dominant reality of this trade-off? At the very least, it would seem important to clarify one's options, grasping how they have been formed and how they might be expanded. At a very simple level, there appears to be only two choices. On the one hand one could focus one's energies on the job, working for changes in job organization and design that might enhance the significance of work in one's life. On the other hand, one might view this as naive or utopian, and opt instead for the intensified but more narrowly focused concern with job payoffs and benefits as a means of supporting personal commitments and the availability of leisure. In either case, the question remains as to how one's agency can be expanded in the face of circumstances that seem to diminish possibilities. The activities in this chapter are intended to be a small step down the road to answering this question.

This chapter consists of the following sections.

- Activity One: Social differences and job satisfaction
- Activity Two: What do you do with your time off the job?
- Activity Three: Housework and the double day
- Activity Four: Making leisure problematic
- Activity Five: Trade-offs
- Activity Six: Having it all

Activity One: Social Differences and Job Satisfaction

This activity will help students explore the systematic relation between work aspirations and satisfaction for people positioned differently in a variety of social relations.

Empirical research into job satisfaction is beset with many pitfalls. Surveys and questionnaires must be carefully devised and results carefully interpreted to shed any light on the complex and often contradictory attitudes people have toward their work. Do they feel satisfaction, for example, with pay, hours of work, security, supervision, work mates, or the work itself? Amid conflicting reports and interpretations, however, there are some consistent findings. One is that differences in job expectations are not random between individuals but are related systematically to categories like social class, gender, and age. Another is that satisfaction is related to expectation and is therefore also related to class, gender, and age. Findings like these are not surprising. For example, older male workers at lower skill and socioeconomic levels often tend to regard their work primarily as a way to earn a living—a means to an end and not an end in itself. They may be satisfied or dissatisfied with the extent to which their jobs fulfill this expectation. Those located in occupations at higher socioeconomic levels (where extrinsic rewards like high pay are taken for granted) expect more in the way of extra-financial, intrinsic rewards in their work.

The activity asks students to consider how differences in job expectations and satisfaction may vary systematically across different groups of people. This may be accomplished by seeing if students can recognize these kinds of patterns in tables and charts of current job satisfaction data, and can interpret the findings of such research.

What to Do in the Classroom

National or local surveys of job satisfaction are regularly done and widely available. Pick one survey that provides extensive charts and tables for students to examine. Make sure the data available include comparisons on social differences such as class, gender, and age.

It will be helpful if students have a clear sense of the meanings of terms commonly used in job satisfaction research. Introduce for discussion and clarification any terms that might be relevant to the survey you will be using as a basis for this activity. Examples of possibly relevant terms are:

• extrinsic rewards: rewards like pay, benefits, and security, which are not part of the actual work being done
• intrinsic rewards: rewards like interest, sense of accomplishment, and development, which are part of the work itself
• aspirations: what people would like as part of their job
• expectations: what people expect to get in a real work situation

Using tables and charts provided by the survey, assign groups of students to answer the following questions on the basis of the data given to them.

1. Who aspires to what? What do young men want from their jobs? What do young women want? How do aspirations change as people get older? What might account for these differences?

2. Who gets what? What kinds of rewards or satisfactions do young men experience at work? What do young women experience? Does the level of reported satisfaction change as people get older? What might account for these differences?

3. What is the relation between aspiration and satisfaction? Does work get better as people get older? Do they lower their aspirations and thereby become more satisfied? Is it a combination of both? Is it the same for men and women? Why or why not?

4. What is the relation between expectation and aspiration? How do age and gender shape expectations?

5. What happens to the answers to these questions when they are compared with those of people who occupy different social class positions?

Teaching Note

The important focus for this exploration and these discussions is the relation between work and life situations. Students should be encouraged to speculate about how it is that age, gender, and social class, together with race, ethnicity, geographic region, and language, shape peoples' aspirations, expectations, and attitudes toward work, in addition to structuring their occupational opportunities.

Students not yet full time in the work force, especially those working in the context of work-study programs, may have a very different relation to job expectations and satisfaction than full-time workers. In relation to their own work experience, have the class answer the survey questions previously examined (see Step 1). Ask students to consider how and why their results might be different from those previously discussed.

Activity Two: What Do You Do with Your Time Off the Job?

Elsewhere we have suggested that students be encouraged to ask their co-workers direct questions related to life on the job (see, for example, Chapter 3 and 4). Here we are interested in exploring the relation between work and non-work activities. We recognize, however, that questions about what people do after work may be more difficult to ask and to legitimate. Certainly in many instances students will have established a rapport with co-workers that allows them access into the personal lives of those with whom they work. At times students may be invited to participate in some forms of non-work activities (e.g., a drink after work, a baby shower, a company picnic, etc.). Very often, however, students will remain outsiders, sometimes owing to their youth, temporary status, or other factors. In such circumstances it is still possible to get a glimpse of the social world beyond the workplace if students listen, pay attention to, and note everyday conversations among co-workers.

What to Do in the Classroom

Have students pay attention to conversations in the workplace—for example, before work, on breaks, at lunch—or ask students to interview a variety of employees more directly. Have them record in their journals which people say what regarding their time off the job. It will be important to see whether they can discover if any relationship seems to exist between what people do at work and how they spend their time off the job. The following questions may be used as a guide for collecting information.

1. From listening to people at work, do you get a sense of what your co-workers do after work? Shop? Housework? Coach a team? Watch television? Read? Take classes? Help with homework? "Just relax?"

2. Do you get a sense of what they do on weekends? Party? Family outings? Housework? Watch television? Play golf? Visit friends and/or relatives?

3. What do they do on vacations? Work overtime? Travel? Fish? Ski? Housework? Go to the cottage? Watch television? Paint the house? "Just relax?"

Either in groups or together with the whole class, collect the information from the journals. Do this by first making a list of all the after-work activities reported to the students. Create a number of categories that will help organize the information. Examples of such categories might include: education, playing sports, consuming popular culture, housework, hobbies, fixing things, family activities, travel. For each time period students have information about (after work, weekends, vacations), have them identify the jobs for which the activity was recorded. Thus, one might ask, "What are the jobs people are doing, for those workers who said they take classes after work? What are the jobs people are doing who say they play sports on the weekend?"

Teaching Note

Point out types of employment that are not represented by the people with whom the students talked. Students may not have had access to a very wide range of people. If this is so, you may wish to assign a few students to try to get information from people in unrepresented jobs.

Note as well that the categorization of information may also be done in relation to differences such as age, gender, and ethnicity. However, if these are included it will be important to help maintain the focus intended here: the relation between work and non-work activities.

The students are now in a position to examine whether the information collected displays any regularities as to the relation between one's work and one's time off the job.

Teaching Note

Here students will be exploring whether or not they think it can be argued that work plays a role in determining the nature of non-work activities. But it is also important to consider the ways in which commitments beyond the workplace might be seen as determining the nature of work opportunities.

Activity Three: Housework and the Double Day

Despite the fact that over half of Canadian married women are in the paid labor force, most wives still retain the major responsibility for childcare and housework. This double burden of work, sometimes called the "double day," is a major factor in determining the amount and quality of time off for wives and mothers in particular and for other household members as well. Much of this domestic labor is "hidden" in the sense that it gets done without being noticed; the toilet bowl doesn't seem to get dirty, clean socks simply appear in drawers. This activity is intended to focus attention on this hidden labor and its distribution within households. It is the first consideration in beginning to make problematic the term "leisure," raising the issue that it is not equally available to all after the day's paid work is done.

What to Do in the Classroom

Have the class generate lists of domestic tasks that need to be done for a household to function. The determination of need will be an interesting problem in itself: Is dusting absolutely necessary? What about walking the dog? Using a frequency table might help to organize this activity. For example:

Daily: make breakfast, prepare lunches, wash dishes, make dinner, help with homework, walk the dog, meal planning.

Weekly: clean the bathroom, do laundry, shop for groceries, put garbage out, cut the grass, change sheets, shovel the driveway, vacuum, drive the kids to swimming/hockey/ballet/work, do the bills.

Seasonally: wash the windows, wrap gifts, get the snow tires put on/taken off, make Thanksgiving dinner, trim the hedge, rake leaves, mend clothing, pack for a trip, attend parent/teacher night.

Annually: shampoo carpets, get the dog's shots, make and take kids to medical/dental appointments, clean the basement/garage/locker, defrost the freezer.

From these general lists, have students develop lists that are appropriate to their specific family situations. On the basis of their own experiences, who does what? What patterns of domestic task allocation are evident?

Once this information is collected, have students consider whether their families overall conform to typical gender stereotypes? In addition, the following questions can be raised. How is this division of domestic labor justified or rationalized in the family? In the culture? Does it make a difference if the mother works outside the home? Does it make a difference if the father is out of work? What happens in sole-support households? Do teenage sons and daughters participate in domestic work equally?

Have students discuss what they anticipate in terms of the division of domestic labor in their own future households? Are men's and women's expectations congruent or contradictory? What are the implications of the views students hold for their own orientations toward work in the future?

Activity Four: Making Leisure Problematic

As we began to show in Activity 3 leisure is not an unproblematic concept. Typically, leisure refers to activities done in one's spare time. However, the very possibility of leisure is dependent not only on how many hours of the day one spends in paid employment but also on issues such as the organization of domestic labor, the income available to purchase auxiliary labor to relieve oneself of chores, and the material and social circumstances available that both provide and limit the range of leisure options possible. Leisure is not something people just have; rather, it is a range of possibilities that are produced, for most people, with a good deal of effort.

Another concern that must be expressed about the concept of leisure is that increasingly our desire for it is being produced by the range of "life-style" or "leisure-time" commodities that are offered for sale. Thus the question needs to be raised as to whether or not the availability of such commodities is shifting people's emphases away from questions of intrinsic job satisfaction to the opportunity for financial remuneration no matter what the substance of work available. If this is so, there may exist an increasing contradiction, which is nicely illustrated by the following statement by a factory worker talking about his leisure time plans.

We bought the camper because we thought it would be a cheap way to get away weekends. There's nothing I like more than going up to Clear Lake with the family—fishing, swimming. But Christ, I've been working every Saturday for the last sixteen months, so there's no chance to use the damn thing. Don't get me wrong. We're not complaining about the overtime. We sure need it. There's lots of bills to pay around this place that just wouldn't get paid without it. (Sighing with perplexity) I guess you can't win. If I had the time to get out of here, there wouldn't be any money.[1]

What to Do in the Classroom

In order to introduce the notion that leisure is something that is produced within a particular set of circumstances, ask students to write down any factors that they think limit or provide their access to leisure-time activities. These may be availability of time and money but may also include things like the location of one's neighborhood or regulations imposed, or not imposed, by parents. Using suggestions from the class, make a list of such factors on the board.

Some of these factors will apply to almost everyone in the class (e.g., homework requirements), while others will be quite particular to certain groups of students (e.g., students from low-income families working to help support family income). Such differences need to be understood in order to begin to comprehend how the opportunities for leisure are systematically structured. From the list generated by the students, ask students to discuss whose opportunities for leisure are more limited and who has more opportunities available. Write these suggestions on the board and pose the question directly if the class has not already raised the issue: How is a person's social class, gender, ethnicity, or regional location a factor in the production of particular life circumstances and constraints on leisure time activity?

Teaching Note

The intention of such discussion is not to focus on the particular circumstances of individual students in the class. Rather, it is to consider how opportunities for leisure are produced and differentially distributed. For example, the restrictions on access to leisure activities would likely be different for a female student of a low-income, immigrant family living outside of the metropolitan area than they would for a male student from a professional family living in a downtown townhouse.

Once the idea that leisure is not something that is equally available to all has been established, it will be possible to consider what students view as the consequences of living within the contradictory space of the commodification of leisure. Have students write a variety of activities that they have done or would like to do in their leisure time. Collect these activities on the board. Have students note which of these activities must be purchased. Then have students discuss how the necessity of purchasing these activities limits the opportunities available to engage in those very same activities. Students should be encouraged to share how they handle these experiences of contradiction.

Teaching Note

Teachers might find it useful to introduce the quotation by the factory worker which is included in the introduction to this activity for class discussion as a way of linking student experiences of contradiction to those often prevalent in adult life.

Activity Five: Trade-Offs

Most of us will have to face the problem of trying to find a job with an acceptable balance of intrinsic and extrinsic rewards. Many people argue that finding an acceptable trade-off between these two goals is simply a "fact of life," given the jobs available in our economy. The design of work, structure of authority, politics of control, and patterns of satisfaction are determined by the scientific, technological, and organizational "advances" of a continuing Industrial Revolution and there-fore what is available in the way of work is beyond the control of the individual worker. In addition, we are often told there is a benefit to all this. That is, efficiency and high productivity benefit *all* society by con-tributing to an overall rise in the standard of living.

There are, however, several alternatives to this technologically deter-ministic view. There are those, for example, who have challenged the fully instrumental approach to work and called for increased employee participation in decision-making. They have argued that this can in fact be done without sacrificing economic values and can even lead to higher productivity (see the discussion of quality of working life in Chapter 4).

Others have suggested that the implementation of new technologies, while oriented to the economic ends of productivity and profitability, may, as an unintended consequence, create more interesting and in-trinsically satisfying jobs.

Still others have encouraged the adoption of smaller, more humane, and environmentally sound technologies and organizational structures within which more interesting and challenging work could be provided. Some supporters of this approach claim that this could be done without loss of efficiency or abundance of goods and services. Others concede that the material standard of living would be lower but the quality of life for everyone would improve (see "Scenarios" in Chapter 13).

In a society in which an instrumental approach to work is taken for granted and where leisure-time commodities fuel the desire for an in-crease in spendable income, is there any demand for increased intrinsic value in work? Would people aspire to self-fulfillment at work if it came at the expense of financial rewards? Or is it the case that most people want to retain and improve their standard of living at the cost of fore-going actualization at work?

What to Do in the Classroom

Have students ask their fellow employees to rank order the following in terms of their own preferences:

• shorter hours of work

• better pay and benefits

• expanded authority and responsibility (enriched job content)

In class, tabulate the results something like this:

Hours	*Pay*	*Job Content*
1st	1st	1st

2nd	2nd	2nd
3rd	3rd	3rd

Relate these findings to the positions discussed in the introduction to this activity. Using their experiences of life on the job, have students discuss their understandings of why people express the preferences they do.

Have students discuss the following statement, giving reasons as to why they agree or disagree with its author:

It is surely a perfectly legitimate preference for people to accept a sacrifice of personal fulfillment at work in order to derive larger economic resources for pursuing personal fulfillment outside work. . . . Indeed, the fact that so many people do not aspire to self-actualization in work may be a fortunate thing. . . . Should we say, "Thank God for the number of people who have made an apparent adjustment to routine jobs. Would that there were more"? Perhaps . . . it would be best to devote our resources to ever-shortening the work week and helping people to enjoy their leisure more fully.[2]

Activity Six: Settling for Less or Having It All?

Why do people indicate that they realize that "work as it is" is something less than "work as it might be," and yet adapt to existing circumstances too often by compromising their own aspirations? Lillian Rubin reports a conversation she had with a 27-year-old warehouseman who, after talking at some length about the business he hoped to have someday, remarks:

After all that talk, I really doubt I'll ever make any change. I'll probably stay where I am forever. Once you've been on the job seven years, look at what you'd have to give up—good money, good benefits, seniority. What if I tried my own business and it didn't work? Then I'd have to come back and start all over again. No, I don't think I'll ever take that chance.[3]

Rubin comments:

Paradoxically, then, the "good money, good benefits, seniority" that come with long tenure on the job also serve to limit his choices—to bind him to it, trading the dream for this stagnant stability. Perhaps, in the long run, that makes sense. . . . In the immediate moment, there's pain and pathos when, at twenty-seven, he already knows his life choices largely are over. [This is] not [a] personal failing, [an] outgrowth of character or personality deficiency. [It is], instead, [a] realistic response to the social context in which most working-class men, women, and children live, grow, and come to define themselves, their expectations, and their relationship to the world around them.[4]

While we would not condone an approach that encourages students to settle for less, neither do we want to mislead them with the promise of unlimited possibility. Contrary to media hype, it may not be possible to "have it all"—rewarding job, good pay, charming spouse, loving kids, interesting friends, inner peace, and a "German-engineered road sedan." Personal aspirations, job expectations, and family responsibilities often conflict: hairdressers work holidays and weekends when the rest of the family gets together; night school is at night, and people work second shift; sales reps travel; jobs require relocation; office buildings make people sick and grouchy.

While having it all might not be possible, having more certainly is if the structures that limit possibilities are removed and replaced with more enabling forms and practices.

What to Do in the Classroom

Have students brainstorm about the kinds of changes they would like to see in the way opportunities for work, love and leisure are made available in society—changes that would enable them to be more and have more by opening up possibilities for accommodating the demands of personal, occupational, and domestic life. To get students started, ask them to consider such social innovations as paid maternity/paternity leave, year-round schooling, paid educational leave, workplace childcare, flex-time, and job sharing. Focus discussion on how these might restructure social relations at work and provide an expanded set of life possibilities for people.

NOTES

1. Lillian Rubin, *Worlds of Pain* (New York: Basic Books, 1976) p. 200.
2. Alan Fox, "The Meaning of Work," in G. Esland, and G. Salaman (eds), *The Politics of Work and Occupation* (Toronto: University of Toronto Press, 1980), p. 188.
3. Rubin, ibid., p. 163.
4. Rubin, ibid., p. 163.

9

Unions: Solving Problems by Sticking Together

Throughout this book we have stressed that work education is not just a method of job training or socializing students to the "work world." Work education must be grounded in the educational agenda of helping students to understand current realities so as to be able to transform them.

Within this perspective, what should students know and understand about labor unions? To begin with, we suggest a basic shift in the way labor unions are normally discussed and studied. We usually talk about unions as if they were some object or thing that could be understood apart from the everyday practical action of people. However, in this chapter the concept of unions will always refer to a concrete interplay of human activities. The following teaching suggestions are designed to help students understand the notion of union as it refers to particular actions a group of people take to improve specific aspects of their everyday lives.

The study of unions suggested in this chapter has the dual purpose of introducing students to some basic information about what unions do and confronting students with the challenge of identifying and assessing both the possibilities and problems associated with the practice of collective action. This perspective is justified by our premise that some current realities that need changing cannot be addressed by individuals working alone; at times notions of solidarity and collective action are called for.

In this chapter we are suggesting that the notion of union be studied as a way in which workers have responded and can respond to the desire for a better life. We take the view that unions as a form of collective action solve problems but may also create some. We have not intended our material to be a form of union advocacy but rather we have chosen to confront students with the reality that much of what takes place in the workplace is a question of choice and value as to the ways in which our working lives will be spent.

It is our assumption that what a union is (as a specific form of collective action) has been and will continue to be the outcome of a struggle, given current economic and social arrangements that foster contradictory interests between workers and management. This struggle has been over how to define the substance and conditions of work in Canadian society. Who should control the terms on which working people live their everyday lives and exactly what should such terms be? Such disputes we assume take place between people who, while they may share many compatible and complementary values and viewpoints, have at least some contradictory beliefs and interests.

In this context, unions refer to a particular set of actions working people have taken to both express their views on such issues and to bring these views into reality. The legitimacy of such actions have not always been accepted by some Canadians. Indeed, the right of people to come together to initiate various forms of direct collective action has been challenged both in the courts and in the streets. This means that a union is the outcome of both a historical and ongoing controversy over what forms of collective action are legitimate in our society. What notion of union is proper for our Canadian society is a question still being raised and contested!

It should be noted that the perspective and activities of this chapter are different from many available curricula on unions and the labor movement. Commonly, most such curricula try to present the "straight facts" pertaining to labor history and/or labor law (usually together with a case study of an organizing drive or a simulation of negotiations or a grievance procedure). Such material can be of considerable interest if a teacher is planning an extensive study of unions. Our suggestions below assume a rather short unit. We have tried to develop material adaptable to approximately three in-class sessions or the equivalent of three to five hours of class time. We have also emphasized activities that investigate aspects of students' own work experience.

This chapter is organized as follows:

• Theme I: Considering collective action

  Activity One: Experiences of "sticking together"

  Activity Two: The farmer's dilemma

- Theme II: Unions as a form of collective action

  Activity Three: What unions actually do

  Activity Four: Unions—who benefits?
- Theme III: Unions—A practice defined through struggle

  Activity Five: Some labor history

  Activity Six: Case study—A contemporary challenge to what is proper union activity

THEME I: CONSIDERING COLLECTIVE ACTION

As made explicit in the introduction to this chapter, unions are considered as a form of collective action. The first two activities of this chapter are intended to sensitize students to some of the complexities and dilemmas often associated with collective action and to provide a framework within which students can investigate the justification, merits, and limitations of particular forms of union activity.

Teaching Note

The topic of unions and the benefits and limitations of collective action can generate considerable emotional response and personal reaction. While this chapter begins with the premise that collective action is often necessary in order to change current realities that need changing, it is important to stress that the chapter does not assume unions to be the only desirable form of collective action, neither does it assume that collective action is unproblematic. Indeed, if teaching from this chapter simply amounts to a form of advocacy of Canadian unionism, much of the educational intent of our suggestions will be lost. For this reason we wish to stress that teachers place considerable emphasis on the complexities and dilemmas associated with collective action as these are made manifest in the discussions generated by the activities that follow.

Activity One: Experiences of "Sticking Together"

One way of introducing the idea of collective action is to begin by referring students to their own experiences.

What to Do in the Classroom

Ask students to prepare for an initial discussion of collective action by providing instructions similar to the following:

This activity requires you to think about your own experience. This includes not only events in school, among friends, or at work that you personally have participated in, but also books you have read, stories you have heard, and films or television programs you have seen.

Try to remember a problem that needed solving or a situation that needed changing where the action required could not be done by people acting on their own, but only by people sticking together and acting collectively.

During class ask students to describe their situations and give their views of the gains and costs to the people involved as a result of acting as they did. Use this discussion to clarify some of the characteristics of collective action.

Teaching Note

By the phrase "people sticking together," we are not only referring to situations within which a division of labor and coordination of efforts is required, but also situations in which the agent of action becomes the group, thus requiring the temporary subordination of individual needs and interests. The key concept to be explored in this context is the notion of solidarity. The word "solidarity" has become so overused that it now smacks of rhetorical jingoism. But it still refers to a basic condition often necessary for empowering people toward a society of expanded possibility. If possible, during discussion try to give an example from your experience.

A caution, however, is warranted. While some students may have experienced "sticking together" in the context of fund-raising activities or even forms of student direct action such as cafeteria boycotts, others in the class may associate "sticking together" with activities that result in unjust forms of exclusion and abuse. While it may be uncomfortable, a full range of experiences should be explored and the opportunity should be taken to stress that solidarity is not a value in and of itself.

Activity Two: The Farmer's Dilemma

To further develop the notion that collective action or "sticking to-gether" is not always easy to maintain and at times may involve a difficult choice among competing values, introduce the following short activity.[1]

What to Do in the Classroom

Organize students into groups of three and ask each group to play the following game. One student will be the referee while the other two play. The players sit back to back so as to not see each other and should not speak to each other during play. Designate each person as either Player 1 or Player 2. The referee controls the game. The game is as follows:

You both are wheat farmers. Each year you have the following two options:

you may grow as much wheat as you can, or you may limit production and grow only a portion of what your land could actually yield.

How much you are able to sell your wheat for will depend on how much wheat is available in the marketplace. Generally, the more wheat available the lower will be the price per bushel and thus you will make less money on your sale. You will get a chance to make decisions over a number of years. Now it is time to make your first decision. Write down your designation as either Player 1 or Player 2 and whether you are going to produce as much as you can ("full") or whether you will limit production ("limit"). Submit your decisions to the referee (who represents the market).

The referee takes these decisions and, on the basis of the following chart, determines how much each player will receive. The referee then writes the result for each player and provides them with the outcomes of their first year decision. He or she then asks for the decision for the next year.

Referee's Chart

- Player 1 and Player 2 both restrict production. Each receives $10,000 for the sale of their wheat.
- Player 1 restricts production and Player 2 produces at full capacity. Player 1 receives $2,000; Player 2 receives $15,000.
- Player 1 produces to full capacity and Player 2 restricts production. Player 1 receives $15,000 and Player 2 receives only $2,000.
- Both Players 1 and 2 produce to full capacity. Both receive $5,000 on the sale of their wheat.

Do not tell the class how long the game should be played. However, let the groups continue to make year by year decisions—giving their choices to the referee and receiving the results—until they have completed ten years.

After the play is finished, it is important that there be some class discussion regarding the decision-making of each pair. Differences among the groups should be noted and students should be encouraged to express the thoughts they had during the play of the game. Specifically, students should be encouraged to express the strategies they used to play the game and the reaction and responses they had to the behavior of the other player.

Teaching Note

This game is structured to explore a dilemma. At any given moment you can do better if you act to maximize your individual short-term gains; however, over the long run this is a less effective strategy. Thus at each moment of decision it pays for a player to "defect" from collective action. However, if both players act this way over the long run they will not do as well as they would if they worked together. In this way the game illustrates clearly the instability of many forms of collective action in which there are immediate short-term benefits available if one acts for oneself at the expense of others. Ask students if they can give examples of this dynamic at work in other contexts.

THEME II: UNIONS AS A FORM OF COLLECTIVE ACTION

A way to begin the consideration of unions as a type of collective action is to start with students' experiences and perceptions of what unions do. Often high school students know very little about what unions do but nevertheless have negative attitudes toward the union movement. It is not unusual to hear students assert that unions are selfish, restrict opportunity for youth, and curtail individual freedom. However, many students also believe that unions are a beneficial way workers can act to protect themselves and enhance their self-interests.

To provide a sense of what attitudes and beliefs about unions one might hear in a class discussion, consider these examples of how one group of students responded to the open-ended statement: "I think unions. . . .":

I think unions
• are useful unless out of control
• help workers
• are a negative aspect of our society
• are good in some ways, getting higher wages and, protecting workers from dangerous working conditions
• can hold you back and work against you
• are good
• are a rip-off
• won't let you think as an individual
• are something I don't know much about

Such responses are rather vague and non-specific but they can serve as an excellent starting point for an in-depth study of unions as a form of collective action.

Activity Three: What Unions Actually Do

Getting Started

Ask students to complete the sentence "I think unions. . . ." Encourage them to respond by drawing on their work experiences (both within work-experience programs or part-time after school), what they have heard about unions from friends and relatives, and their perceptions from the media. After a few minutes students are then asked to share their responses with the class. The teacher records a list of between eight to ten responses on chart paper or a blackboard without interrupting or asking students for clarification. This is important because the next step in this activity requires the use of this record.

Being Specific

Once this is done the class as a whole should be asked to be more specific and list what unions actually do that would justify the assertion(s) made in each sentence. For example, if someone has said "I think unions are useful unless out of control," ask students to specify what unions do that are useful and what they do when they get out of control. The point here is to acknowledge the attitudes and initial understandings students have of unions and to frame an inquiry into what unions actually do. As in the first step, the teacher again makes a public record (on the blackboard or on chart paper) of the student responses. This time a list is made of all the union activities students can think of given their current understanding of what unions actually do. The length and accuracy of this list will vary from class to class but such variations are not a concern. The list just defines a starting point for learning.

Going beyond Past Experience

Now it is time to test the adequacy of this initial understanding by asking students to go beyond the limits of their past experience. In this activity students are asked to go beyond their past experiences in two different ways: by talking to people they have not previously met and by reading accounts of other people's experiences of union activities. This should be done by assigning specific interviewing and reading responsibilities to particular students. In both cases the objective is to see if the initial list of activities generated in the second step above is accurate and comprehensive.

Teaching Note

In a workplace where there is a union, students should be asked to meet and talk with union representatives in order to find out the range of activities the union is involved in. If possible, some students should be assigned to visit union offices and workplaces other than their placement sites and talk with union representatives about the activities that comprise their unions.

It is important that students read a range of articles describing various types of union activity in addition to talking to workers, management, and union officials. Gather or assign the task of gathering a range of materials that describe what unions actually do. Be sure to gather readings that present a broad and comprehensive description of union activity. For example, we suggest that material be gathered that describes union efforts to:

- *prevent plant closures*
- *improve health and safety conditions at work*
- *organize wage settlements and collective agreements*
- *promote anti-racism and anti-sexism activities*
- *supply social benefits: housing co-ops, legal aid, medical services and insurance*
- *participate in political activity*
- *supply aid to developing countries*

By emphasizing this range of activities we are suggesting that a view of union activity be presented that is squarely within the Canadian tradition of "social unionism." We recognize that both within and outside of the union movement this notion of "union" is being challenged. This challenge will be the focus of the learning activities specified in Theme III of this chapter.

Once a comprehensive set of materials is collected, organize the distribution of this material in order to ensure that all students will have read at least one short account of union activities in each of the above areas.

Consolidating Learning

After information is gathered the students should be asked to evaluate the adequacy of their initial understanding of unions. This requires going back to the assertions and lists generated in the second step above and considering the contrast between what personal experience and "common knowledge" provided in the way of understanding what unions do, and what is suggested by student research and reading. If students' initial understanding (as expressed in the second step) was limited or seemingly biased in some way, it will be important for the students to consider why this was so, and why their previous experiences gave them a limited understanding.

Teaching Note

This is important! You will be asking students to consider what it is that shapes the limits of their own knowledge. The point is to help students gain some insight into how the limitations of personal experience can result from the systematic distortion of information or exclusion of some people from sources of information. Once this question is raised and discussed it is important to follow with a consideration of why such exclusion or distortion has happened and who benefits and loses from this state of affairs.

Activity Four: Unions—Who Benefits?

We suggest that this theme be concluded by considering the desirability and limitations of different forms of union activity as examples of collective action.

What to Do in the Classroom

Return to the reconsidered list of activities that describes what unions actually do (see Activity 3, "Consolidating Learning") and ask students to consider the benefits and liabilities of each type of collective action: to union members, to management, to the general public, and to the students themselves.

In addition, have students consider the implications of any of the various forms of collective action discussed for their workplaces. What do they think might be accomplished? What constraints or reasons exist that would limit the viability of people acting collectively at work?

Teaching Note

This discussion may provoke some heated debate and several topics that some members of the class may wish to explore further. One issue that should be raised in discussion is whether or not union activities benefit only union members or whether all workers benefit from union accomplishments. Another issue that should be raised is whether union–management relations necessarily involve questions of competing rights: for example, business property rights, the right to a fair wage, community rights. Another question is whether actions such as job security clauses in collective agreements restrict job opportunities for youth trying to enter the labor force.

THEME III: UNIONS—A PRACTICE DEFINED THROUGH STRUGGLE

What should be the legitimate function of unions and what aspects of our lives should they influence? These questions are vital to many of us whether or not we work in the home, in an office or factory, a small company, or a large corporation. Such questions are by no means new. In Canada they have been central to the history of the labor movement and have been a source of much disagreement and argument not only within that movement but also between workers and owners/management. By introducing students to these questions we want to stress the following:

1. What a union is or does is not a question of fact but a contentious issue that has not yet been resolved. Arguments for one position or another regarding what notion of union is proper for Canada are grounded in preferences and

values. Thus what a union is or does cannot be presented as a fact (e.g., such as the statement, "Schomberg is 35 kilometers from Toronto"). Rather it must be understood as a historical and social construction that is constantly being challenged, affirmed, and modified.

2. At any given moment in history the range of activities that are considered legitimate union activities is the outcome of struggle between groups of people with opposing commitments and values structured by particular social histories and relations.

3. Particular forms of collective action on the part of any group may be opposed by others. This opposition needs to be understood, assessed, and resolved if the quality of everyday life is to be maintained and improved.

Activity Five: Some Labor History

For most Canadians today the existence of unions is taken for granted. In Canada approximately 35 percent of our labor force are members of unions. Indeed, most of us would be surprised to learn that just a little over 100 years ago unions were illegal in Canada. Unions were considered illegal conspiracies and unlawful forms of collective action. Prior to 1872 union members were often prosecuted under the Master and Servant Act for joining with others to demand "extravagant and high wages."

Activity Four of this chapter stressed the wide range of actions that today forms a spectrum of lawful activities that are collectively undertaken within unions. Thus the history of labor unions in Canada is the history of the legitimation of a developing perspective from which working people can act collectively to improve the quality of life for themselves, their families, and their communities. But this perspective did not simply emerge out of thin air; neither was it accepted by everyone. The development of this perspective is rooted in the particular history of the relationship between workers and owners/management in Canada.

This perspective is still not accepted by everyone. It is still being challenged in offices, factories, and in the courts. This means that the notion of unions as it occurs in today's work world is not static but the continual outcome of a struggle between different interests and points of view over what constitutes desirable forms of collective action.

The two activities of Theme III require historical study. It may be surprising to some that we have included historical study in an experientially oriented curriculum concerned with the world of work. However, in our view such study is essential. As we have continually restated, our position is that educating students means helping them to understand necessity so as to transform it. From this perspective we argue that students should never be asked to accept "what is" in the world as simply given, even though at times it may be strategic to act "as if" this were the case. Rather, students should always be encouraged to ask why things are the way they are. History is important to this educational standpoint because it can raise both the question, "How did things get to be this way?" and its correlate, "What would have to be done for things to be otherwise?" The point here is that it is important for us to grasp how human actions patterned over time are the source of our current social structures and institutional practices. In this way we can begin to get a sense of how some of the real, objective constraints on our daily lives are historical (not given, not natural) and hence open to change.

Teaching Note

History is not inherently interesting to all students. Indeed, many of us have confronted people with a marked indifference toward the past. For effective teaching of Activities Five and Six it would be best if students could address these activities from the vantage point of their own personally posed historical questions. When such questions are posed as a result of prior work experiences, discussion, and reading, they are excellent starting points for historical inquiry. We suggest that the teacher make note of such questions (e.g., I wonder how it got to be that way?) as may arise at any point during the teaching of the material offered in this book. Such questions can then be a concrete beginning for the study of history, which becomes more than an obligatory reference to what is seen as an irrelevant past.

What to Do in the Classroom

Teachers should acquire some of a variety of readable materials that describe union history in Canada. In particular this material should include as discussion of J. S. Woodward and the notion of social unionism, the Social Alliance, and the development of the Rand formula.[2]

Beyond having students read and discuss one or more of the resources for historical study students may be asked to:

1. Use the historical material to develop a questionnaire for an "historical awareness" survey. This survey can be given to parents, co-workers, teachers, people in the street, and so on to document the degree of historical awareness people have about labor unions in Canada. Where students uncover substantial ignorance about this segment of Canadian history it will be important to raise and discuss the problems associated with this form of social amnesia—that is, why so little is known about labor history.

2. From the readings gathered for Activity Four and the historical resources available for Activity Five, have students develop a list of actions used in the struggle between labor and owners/management. Ask them to identify different forms of legal action, work action, and political action. The point here is not only to ensure that students understand the meaning of various terms often used to describe the tactics of union–management relations but also to appreciate how struggle is actually carried out. (For example, on the labor side: court actions, support for labor-oriented legislation, strikes, slowdowns, work to rule, factory occupations, certification campaigns, alliances with other social movements. On the owner/management side: court actions, support for business- and management-oriented legislation, lockouts, speedups, plant closings, introduction of technology that de-skills and displaces workers, regulation and monitoring of workers by machines, de-certification campaigns.)

3. Pose the questions: Why did Canadian businessmen think union activity was a crime? Were the owners just greedy or were the workers threatening the foundations of "peaceful society"? Have groups use the resources for historical study to develop improvised dramatic portrayals that provide answers to these questions. Have various groups discuss the different interpretations given in the dramas.

4. The term "scab" is used to name someone who crosses a picket line to take a union member's job while she or he is on strike. Ask students to explain why this term is so emotionally loaded and to contrast it with the management term "replacement worker," also used to name someone who crosses the picket line. Canadian Prime Minister Brian Mulroney in the context of a recent postal strike said that no Mulroney ever crossed a picket line to scab and he would not countenance it now. Ask students to dramatize a confrontation between union members and scabs so that the point of view of each party is explained. Ask them to be sure to include an explanation of the underlying conditions that set people up into such hostile confrontations.

Activity Six: Case Study—A Contemporary Challenge to What is Proper Union Activity in *Lavigne v. OPSEU*

Lavigne v. OPSEU (Ontario Public Service Employees Union) is a contemporary challenge to existing notions of what activities a union may legitimately engage in. It demonstrates that notions of proper union activity is still contested in Canada. The case provides a rich set of issues that are useful for both reviewing basic information about unions and consolidating students' understanding of the complexities of collective action.

Accompanying materials contain:

• introduction to the Lavigne case

• Lavigne files suit

• NCC—a test case

• the arguments

• Judge White's decision

What to Do in the Classroom

The class is asked to role play an appeal court considering the Lavigne case. Students are divided into three groups. One group will be the appeal court judges. Another group will develop and argue the case for Merve Lavigne—that Judge White's decision should be upheld. The final group will develop and argue the case for OPSEU and the OFL (Ontario Federation of Labor), asking that Judge White's decision be overturned. Judge White's decision was:

that compulsory dues may only be used for the purpose which justifies their imposition and for no other purpose beyond that. In other words, the use of compulsory dues for purposes other than collective bargaining and collective agreement administration cannot be justified in a free and democratic society, where the individual objects to such use. (Justice White's decision, *Lavigne v. OPSEU*)

Students in all three groups should study the issues involved in this case prior to the mock appeal trial. Students should be encouraged to use not only the arguments supplied in the case material but any other information or viewpoints they have developed during the study of this unit. Students might also be encouraged to solicit views from employers and employees in their workplaces. The teacher should help groups consider whether people's views on this case are related to their personal work histories.

THE CASE: *LAVIGNE V. OPSEU*

Introduction

A recent court case has highlighted conflicting opinions about the role of unions in Canadian society. The case, which received prominent coverage in the press, pitted an Ontario community college teacher named Merve Lavigne and a lobby group named the National Citizens Coalition (NCC) against one of the largest public sector unions in the country, the Ontario Public Service Employees Union (OPSEU).

Lavigne and the NCC initiated the court action against OPSEU to challenge its right to use his dues money for political purposes, including support for the New Democratic Party, with which he did not agree. The legal arguments centered on OPSEU's right to collect dues from

Lavigne and its use of this money. But the issues involved in the conflict were of much broader significance than this.

Lavigne and the NCC claimed to be acting in the interests of individual workers against "big unions" which, they claimed, have grown too powerful. The NCC saw the court case as a step toward its aim of limiting union activities to negotiating and overseeing collective agreements. By challenging OPSEU's use of Lavigne's dues money, they hoped to take away the financial ability of unions to participate in political and social movements.

OPSEU and the labor groups that supported it claimed that Lavigne and the NCC were trying to benefit business interests by weakening the labor movement. They argued that the laws that allowed OPSEU to collect dues from Lavigne and use this money for political purposes were a recognition that unions must be active outside as well as inside the workplace in order to represent workers. They were fighting to defend a tradition of "social unionism" which, they claimed, has made life better for Canadian workers.

The Local Dispute: Lavigne and OPSEU Local 653

The Lavigne case is important because it affects the future of the Canadian labor movement and the relationship between all workers and employers in Canada. But, like most issues of national significance, it started as a local dispute involving real people in the town of Haileybury, Ontario.

Haileybury is now a small town 160 kilometers north of North Bay. But in the early part of this century, during a boom in silver mining, Haileybury was a flourishing center for managers employed by the big mining companies. Here, the managers built large lakeshore homes and raised their families a respectable distance away from the mines. Meanwhile, the miners and their families lived in the nearby town of Cobalt, surrounded by mine shafts, tailings, and other debris.

Haileybury once had the only high school in the area. The big mining companies also built a school of mining in Haileybury. After World War II the Haileybury School of Mines became established as a world leader in technical training for hard-rock mining. Many of its graduates, who include Merve Lavigne, went on to become mine managers.

Merv Lavigne began a teaching job at the Haileybury School of Mines after it became part of the provincial community college system in the 1960s. The shift from a school run by private mining companies to a publicly operated college involved changes that are important in Lavigne's dispute with the Ontario Public Service Employees Union (OPSEU).

As a teacher at a provincial college, Lavigne became a public employee.

Along with thousands of other Ontario government workers, he was represented by OPSEU.

An act of the provincial legislature recognizes OPSEU as the only legitimate representative of college teachers in negotiations with the provincial government. Like a small minority of government workers, Lavigne chose not to join the union. But, following the Rand formula, he was required to pay dues to OPSEU.

For many years, Lavigne's status as a dues-paying non-member of OPSEU Local 653 seemed acceptable to both parties. Lavigne shared in the wage increases and benefits negotiated by the union. He had as much right as a member to vote on contracts and strikes, and to be represented by the union in grievances with his employer. To support this work, the union received from Lavigne dues equal to the dues paid by union members. This is the arrangement set out by the Rand formula to prevent "free riding" by non-members of unions. The dispute between Lavigne and OPSEU began in 1984, during the first faculty strike in the community college system. In the fall of that year negotiations between OPSEU and the provincial government broke down over workload issues. Teachers at Ontario's 22 community colleges, including Haileybury School of Mines, voted to reject the government's contract offer and go on strike.

Lavigne objected to the strike. He called the striking teachers "radical jerks" and, supported by managers of the large mines, set up a group called the Committee for Responsibility in Education to oppose the strike. Along with several other teachers, Lavigne crossed the picket line to continue teaching at Haileybury School of Mines.

OPSEU brought a complaint against Lavigne before the Labour Relations Board for working during the strike. In response, Lavigne attempted legal action to "decertify OPSEU as my bargaining agent." His constitutional rights were violated, Lavigne charged, by the provincial legislation that required him to pay dues and be represented by OPSEU, and prevented the government from paying strike-breaking teachers.

Lavigne's lawsuit was interrupted when, three and one-half weeks into the strike, the government passed legislation to send the teachers back to work. Subsequent negotiations and a major government inquiry led to a contract settlement that was favorable to the teachers' demand for an easing of their workload. But the dispute between Lavigne and OPSEU was far from over. The National Citizens Coalition (NCC) had contacted Lavigne during the strike. Its involvement would significantly shift the focus of Lavigne's complaint and transform the local dispute into a national battle.

The Constitutional Challenge—A Test Case for the NCC

The National Citizens Coalition was founded in 1967 when Colin Brown, a millionaire insurance salesman, placed a newspaper advertisement denouncing universal medicare and asking whether anyone "out there" agreed with him. Since then, the NCC has grown into an influential political lobby group.

Lavigne's views appealed to the people who run the NCC. His statements to the press during the college teachers' strike caught their attention. A few months after the end of the strike the NCC announced that it was supporting Lavigne in a new court challenge under the Canadian Charter of Rights and Freedoms.

A recurring theme in NCC campaigns had been a claim that unions, especially public service unions, are too strong and that they abuse their powers. It had used newspaper ads to denounce public employees' wage demands, and to call for the decertification of the postal workers' union.

The Lavigne case, which soon became the basis for the largest publicity campaign in the history of the NCC, is a more fundamental challenge to the power of unions than were these earlier campaigns. It questioned the role of the entire labor movement in Canadian society. It was "a natural case for the Coalition to take up," said an NCC spokesperson. "We'd been looking for a test case."

"Should unions force Canadians, through compulsory dues, to finance political parties and causes?" This question, which appeared at the top of a full-page advertisement the NCC placed in major daily newspapers, signaled a shift in Lavigne's legal case.

Lavigne maintained the original argument that his right to earn a living had been violated by the law that prevented him from being paid for working during the college teachers' strike. But the main focus of his challenge became whether OPSEU should be able to use dues money from an unwilling contributor to finance activities not directly related to collective bargaining. At issue were payments which, Lavigne charged, OPSEU had made to support various political causes, including the New Democratic Party (NDP), disarmament and anti-Cruise testing groups, a group in favor of more access to abortions, Nicaragua, the British National Union of Mineworkers, and a campaign against spending public money on a domed stadium in Toronto.

Lavigne argued that the provincial laws that forced him, as a non-union member, to pay dues to OPSEU also forced him to unwillingly support these groups. These laws, he charged, were a violation of his freedoms of expression and association as guaranteed in the Charter of Rights and Freedoms.

The object of Lavigne's lawsuit may seem modest. The portion of his annual dues that went to political causes was less than $3—under 1 percent of what he paid to the union each year. Nevertheless, the potential implications of Lavigne's challenge were enormous. At stake were two opposing views of the legitimate role of unions in Canadian society.

Implicit in the arguments of the NCC was the view that labor unions exist only to enable workers to negotiate with their employers for better wages, benefits, and working conditions. According to this view, unions have no business getting involved in political causes that are beyond the scope of the contracts they negotiate with employers.

If the NCC's challenge was successful, OPSEU would be able to use its money only to negotiate and implement collective agreements. And the precedent set by such a ruling could apply not only to OPSEU but to all Canadian unions.

OPSEU argued that the labor movement has always had a much broader role in Canadian society. From the beginning, Canadian unions have worked to improve their members' lives in the community as well as the workplace. For example, unions took a leading role on the campaigns to eliminate child labor, and in the struggles for publicly provided medical care, pensions, and unemployment insurance.

According to this view, unions must be politically active because conditions in the workplace are directly affected by social conditions. Equally important, the well-being of union members is inseparable from that of their families and other workers. OPSEU spokespersons recalled J. S. Woodsworth's words to express this sentiment: "What we desire for ourselves, we wish for all."

OPSEU argued that it was fighting the NCC to defend this Canadian tradition of social unionism. If it lost the case, all unions would be financially hindered from influencing public policy for the benefit of their members and Canadian society in general.

The Arguments

In February 1986, almost a year after the NCC began its campaign in support of Merve Lavigne, its legal challenge reached the Supreme Court of Ontario. Both OPSEU and the NCC hired prominent lawyers to argue their cases before Justice John White.

Lavigne and the NCC aimed to show that certain parts of the law governing collective bargaining in Ontario's community colleges violated Lavigne's freedoms of expression and association. Because these are among the fundamental freedoms guaranteed in the Canadian Charter of Rights and Freedoms, any laws that are shown to violate them are declared invalid. For this reason, the outcome of the case would affect not only OPSEU but all unions and employers that operate under legal provisions similar to those being challenged.

In their submission to the court, Lavigne and the NCC set out in detail their arguments to show that Lavigne's freedoms of expression and association had been violated, that this violation was unjustified, and what remedy should be used to correct this violation.

Lavigne and the NCC directed their court challenge at sections of the

Colleges Collective Bargaining Act that applied the Rand formula to compel college teachers who are not OPSEU members to pay dues to the union. These sections, their lawyers argued, forced Lavigne to associate himself, by paying dues, with the union and the causes that the union supports. And this arrangement limited Lavigne's freedom to express himself and to associate with any groups of his choice.

In making this argument, Lavigne's counsel maintained that the fundamental freedoms guaranteed in the Charter include the right to choose not to associate oneself with any group and not to express oneself. By compelling Lavigne to pay dues to OPSEU, the Colleges Collective Bargaining Act suppressed Lavigne's right not to associate and his right not to express himself.

Lavigne and the NCC did not object to the Rand formula itself. They distinguished between using compulsory dues to support collective bargaining and using them to support other activities. Lavigne and his supporters challenged only the use of compulsory dues for what they defined as "non-collective bargaining activities."

Here, lawyers for Lavigne and the NCC referred to a section of the Charter that allows "reasonable limits" to the fundamental rights and freedoms set out in it. Compulsory payment of union dues to support collective bargaining is justified, they argued in court, because the legal framework for bargaining and administering contracts between unions and employers is a "sound socio-economic compromise."

But support for the NDP and other political causes is not part of collective bargaining, according to Lavigne's position. Therefore, use of compulsory union dues for such "non-collective bargaining" activities was a violation of Lavigne's rights and freedoms under the Charter.

OPSEU argued that there had been no violation of freedoms guaranteed by the Charter. Even if Lavigne's freedoms of expression and association had been suppressed, they added, the use of compulsory dues for political causes was a justifiable limitation of these fundamental freedoms.

Lavigne had chosen not to join OPSEU, and that choice had been respected by the union. He was still free to express his views and had not become associated with the union's political causes because a very small part of his dues were used to support those causes. A union, the OPSEU lawyer argued, has the same right as any other private organization to decide in a democratic way how its money is spent. Therefore, there had been no breach of Lavigne's freedoms.

Even if the judge rejected this argument, OPSEU maintained, the alleged limitations of Lavigne's freedoms of expression and association were justified. OPSEU argued that there is no valid distinction between collective bargaining in the workplace and broader political action. Throughout the history of the Canadian labor movement, unions have engaged in political and social action, as well as collective bargaining, in order to promote their members' interests. To accept Lavigne's separation of collective bargaining and non-collective bargaining activities would be to ignore a long Canadian tradition of social unionism, argued OPSEU.

Judge White's Decision

On July 4, 1986, Justice John White released his decision on the Lavigne case. His ruling on the central issue of the challenge was clearly in favor of Lavigne and the NCC: "The use of compulsory dues for purposes other than collective bargaining and collective agreement administration cannot be justified in a free and democratic society, where the individual objects to such use." Colin Brown, founder of the NCC, declared he was delighted by the decision: "This is an important victory for freedom of the individual. This is history in the making."

OPSEU and other labor groups supporting the union acknowledged the ruling had gone against them. "Accepting this judgment would mean a total reversal of everything working people have strived for," said Canadian Labour Congress (CLC) President Shirley Carr. She announced that the CLC would support OPSEU in an appeal to the Supreme Court of Canada.

NOTES

1. The structure of this game is adapted from "The Prisoner's Dilemma," in R. Duncan Luce and Howard Raiffa, *Games and Decisions* (New York: John Wiley, 1958) pp. 94–102.

2. The Rand Formula refers to the required practice of deducting union dues at source for all members of a bargaining unit whether or not they choose to become members of the union. The principle behind this practice is that members and non-members benefit from the improvements negotiated by the union and should share the cost of collective bargaining.

IV

Exploring Work as an Exchange Relation

10

Self-Assessment: Changing Circumstances, Changing Selves

When I was younger I wanted to be rich. In the eighth grade I wanted to be a doctor or a lawyer or an executive. . . . I'm older and more realistic now.

I changed when I stopped hanging around with a group of friends who were a bad influence.

These two statements by students represent two different ways we tend to account for changes in ourselves. The first emphasizes the notion of maturation—a process that is sometimes taken for granted as a self-explanatory process of development. The second emphasizes that changes in ourselves occur when the circumstances we are in change. This chapter emphasizes the importance of explanations of change that focus on the concrete opportunities available to people at particular points of time in their lives. This view is consistent with our approach to work-study education, which sees it as an opportunity for the discovery and development of new interests and capabilities, feelings about oneself, and understandings of one's relationship to the world. In this chapter it is important that the teacher focus class discussion on how changing circumstances lead to changes in ourselves and what brings about a change in circumstances. This is the key to beginning a discussion of what forms of individual and collective action people can take if they are dissatisfied with their everyday working lives.

CLARIFYING OBJECTIVES: WHAT IS SELF-ASSESSMENT?

There is no simple single answer to the question: What is self-assessment? What it is and why you may wish to include self-assessment activities in your curriculum will depend on which particular set of assumptions and purposes you wish to build into your course. Here are several suggestions that explain why students might be asked to engage in self-assessment activities.

1. Students can do such an assessment in order to help with a career or job choice. The goal is to assess the appropriateness of different types of occupations for a person. We might characterize this goal as helping a person "choose" what types of labor commodity to become. In other words, there is the practical objective of helping students to identify with a particular marketable form of labor. This would be important for anyone who is trying to find a job in today's labor market.

2. Students can do such an assessment in order to help them to define their goals and desires in the context of a rational process of life planning. Here the intent is to clarify thoughts on questions such as: What do I want out of life? What are possible ways of getting it? Which of these ways are possible and appropriate for me? What do I have to do to get started?

3. Students can do such an assessment in order to help define what types of work, working conditions, and social relations would be a desirable basis on which to define their work in the world. Questions addressed under this intention include: What would I like an opportunity to do? How would I like to "be" in relation to others and my environment? What opportunities and constraints currently exist that influence my ability to take up such a position? How can I use these opportunities and alter these constraints?

GUIDANCE OR SOCIAL ANALYSIS OR BOTH?

The above three versions of what purposes might be served by the activity of self-assessment are all oriented to a decision-making process about the future. They are all intended as a source of clarification and an ordering of one's "now" in relation to one's future life. Thus they can be classified in curricular terms as aspects of guidance. In choosing student activities for this chapter we have acknowledged the importance of all three of the above reasons for having students engage in self-assessment activities. However, the first and third versions reflect different assumptions regarding the acceptance of existing dominant definitions of work, occupational requirements, and the purposes of many contemporary work education programs. While we think it is important that young people entering the labor market know how to structure their planning to fit the realities of that market, we also think that our responsibilities as educators require us to help young people consider how they might act individually and collectively to alter the possibilities open to them.

Yet there is another orientation of self-assessment that does not presume (but neither does it exclude) a direct relation with future planning. Such an assessment may be thought of as activities that promote practice in understanding how one's own thoughts and feelings are related to and influenced by the nature of the situations one has been, and is currently, a part of. The purpose here is social analysis. It recognizes that who we are is influenced by the lives we live and it is aimed at helping students understand how types of work and living arrangements regulate who it is people become. This latter aim is an important feature of being able to assess one's relationship to the society in which one lives.

Thus, this chapter also includes activities that are intended to facilitate a self-awareness that ties one's interests, abilities, temperament, and values to existing social arrangements within which people work, learn, play, and live. Here students can begin to consider how they are both created and limited by their particular life circumstances and consider what alternative ways of working and living could be supported by other possible ways of defining one's work in the world. Such a self-assessment is of major educational importance. We think education ought to ask students to evaluate the desirability of existing ways work is made available to them and to consider what it would take for the current world of work to be otherwise.

What this discussion implies is that teachers who structure self-assessment activities for their students should be clear as to what mix of purposes they intend. The activities, assignments, and evaluative suggestions given in this chapter allow for the teacher to construct her or his own mix of purposes. However, as our comments here suggest, we advocate using a combination of activities that span the range of both guidance and social analysis.

Teaching Note

Self-assessment is not the same as self-evaluation; it is not intended as a procedure through which students determine if they are capable or incapable, adequate or inadequate. However, teachers should recognize that any procedure that asks students to assess their fit to the existing labor market is implicitly evaluative in that it assigns students a corresponding monetary worth and social status. In saying this we are simply acknowledging the existence of prevalent social beliefs and values. We recommend that teachers deal with this issue openly and honestly, remembering that students whose future appears limited in the face of existing realities probably do not need to be constantly reminded of this fact (indeed, career fantasies can often reflect the desire to escape these well-

recognized but seldom spoken limitations). What should be stressed where possible is that it is not the individual who is limited but rather the work world. People may have to cope and contend with its realities but they do not have to internalize its limits as negative judgments of their personal worth.

How to Schedule the Activities Suggested in this Chapter

The idea of self-assessment is applicable to the entire length of a course taught under the work-study method. Self-assessment should not be thought of as a theme appropriate only to a student's pre-placement in-class time. As is the case with all the chapters in the book, the content of this chapter contains both activities that can be done independently of student work experiences and activities especially designed to utilize student work experiences as a source of study, description, analysis, and the clarification of a student's future possibilities. This range of suggestions will allow teachers to choose appropriate activities that integrate the notion of self-assessment throughout the entire sequence of a course. In our view, extended work experience can be an important vehicle through which students may learn new things about the relation between themselves and the challenges and responsibilities demanded by the particular jobs they undertake.

The activities contained in this chapter include:

- Activity One: Changes
- Activity Two: Career planning and the use of tests
- Activity Three: Using journal writing for self-assessment
- Activity Four: Other voices—what can be learned from other people's views of their work?
- Activity Five: Job descriptions—is this job right for you?

Activity One: Changes

When people try to understand who they are, what they are interested in, what capabilities they have—whether it is by means of autobiography or psychological test—the result is an account of oneself at a particular moment in time. Events and desires that seemed critical to us ten years ago are barely remembered now, while others barely noticed then have taken on new importance. We change based on what opportunities we've had, who we've met, what we've had to do, and what's become important to us.

This activity is intended to help students see themselves as changing, developing people. It emphasizes that what you are like today can be different from what you were like in the past and what you will be like in the future. While there are continuities in all our lives, it is important in doing self-assessments that students not view themselves as fixed or unchangeable personalities but rather as people who are constantly changing as a result of new experiences.

What to Do in the Classroom

Ask students to consider how their interests and attitudes have changed over the previous seven- to ten-year period. This may be done by having them write down the changes they have experienced in categories such as: what you and your friends like to do together; what music, TV, and films you enjoy; what things you feel you are able to do well; what you would like to do after you finish school. High school students may find it easier to consider such questions in relation to time units such as the present, when they were in grade nine, and when they were in grade six. An older and more varied group of students may be asked to consider such changes in relation to a different series of events or, if necessary, de-contextualized time units such as the present, five years ago, and ten years ago.

Foreshadow for students that this activity is one in which they will get the opportunity to consider what it is that influences the way people change over time. Ask students to look over the list of changes they have described and choose one or two that they are curious about. Then have them write down some ideas on what change in circumstances might have influenced these changes. To make this a bit more specific, you might have them focus on the particular people and events that seem associated with these changes.

Once this is done, ask them to write down a few suggestions as to what would explain how or why their circumstances changed. You might suggest they try to think of reasons that express both things done to them (e.g., their family moved) or they did themselves (e.g., they got a part-time job).

Discuss with the class (or in small groups if the class is too large) how change happens in people's lives. Use examples students provide to make two lists: (1) the reasons why people change; and (2) how changes in circumstances take place. Consider these lists and discuss such issues as: Are some reasons for change more appropriate for women than for men? Are there types of reasons for change that students had no control over? What types of reasons for change will they be able to control in the future?

Have students review their original responses to the questions posed in the first step and choose two of their current interests or attitudes that they expect will have changed five years from now. Ask them to speculate for each choice on the events and people that might influence them to change. Discuss what things will have to happen to them and what things they will have to do to bring these changes about.

Activity Two: Career Planning and the Use of Tests

Today when jobs for young people are scarce and the labor market is complex and changing, teachers and guidance counsellors are increasingly being directed to tailor their efforts toward helping students gain employment after leaving school. This emphasis has resulted in a renewed interest in standardized assessment testing as a basis for career counselling and planning. This renewed interest is in part a result of the assumption that the needs of large numbers of students can be more efficiently addressed through testing and that testing is a viable, scientific procedure, the use of which demonstrates one's accountability to the increasingly frequent request to "do something about career planning."

We do think there is a place for vocational testing in the process of career planning. Indeed, we think it is highly desirable to include tests in work-education courses that focus on objectives such as self-awareness and career decision-making. However, a place for vocational tests can only be granted if both the benefits and limitations of tests are understood by teachers and the students who use the test results. It is the students who must comprehend the test results and integrate them into their decisions about the course of their future lives. Young people who seek help in gaining employment, whether from a government employment center, a school counselling service, or a private or community employment agency, are likely to face the request (and sometimes the requirement) to take a vocational test as part of a program of counselling and placement. They should as much as possible know what a test is, how it is interpreted, and what its benefits and liabilities are.

We have included a brief summary of the purposes and structure of tests that teachers may use for their own understanding and as a basis for a class session with their students. In what follows we shall briefly state our own point of view regarding the major limitations and benefits of vocational testing and then suggest several activities teachers may employ in helping students gain an informed perspective on the use of tests in career planning. (The following discussion is based on Liz Sayer and Audrey Swail, *Sex Bias in Vocational Testing*) (Toronto, Ontario: *Ontario Women's Directorate*, 1983.)

Why Worry about Vocational Tests?

Assessment through standardized tests presumes one can describe an individual's essential characteristics in terms of "facts" elicited through questionnaires. When employed by a teacher or counsellor, such tests become a tool in assisting students to identify aspects of themselves that indicate a potential career direction or suitability for a particular job. The greatest danger in testing is the tendency for those who use tests to assume that they are objective and "scientific," and hence immune to error and systematic bias. As experienced and informed users of tests acknowledge, such an assumption is false. There is the possibility of error and bias in all four areas of testing used for assessments for career decision-making: interest inventories, ability and aptitude assessments, personality and temperament inventories, and values clarification instruments.

Why Use Tests?

We have suggested above that teachers should incorporate tests as a component of a self-assessment unit simply because vocational testing is so prevalent that students ought to know something about it. However, there is more to it than this. In any self-assessment it is important to make use of a person's past experiences to evaluate one's likes and dislikes, strengths and weaknesses. If we stop there and only use these experiences, however, we will have introduced a problem. As each person only has a small and socially limited realm of experience from which to draw, we need to find other methods of reflection that expand one's scope of possibilities and perhaps uncover hidden interests or aptitudes. To the extent that vocational tests help students to do this, they can be educationally useful.

What to Do in the Classroom

The following three activities focus primarily on ways to help students gain a perspective on how to use vocational tests. Tests are supposed to "bring order to the chaos, frustration and confusion many people experience in making decisions about the future at work" (Sayer and Swail, *Sex Bias*, p. 8). They do this by sampling a small bit of student behavior (mainly by getting students to respond to questions) and then ordering this behavior into a framework for discussion and exploration (usually by mapping students' behavior onto supplied scales or dimensions). The activities below also employ tests as a framework for discussion and exploration.

The teacher picks a standardized interest inventory for the class to use. We recommend that teachers use relatively short forms—any commonly used test is possible. The purpose of this activity is to have students assess the nature of the ambiguities they feel as they respond to test items. Students are then to work on and with this test critically. They are not so much taking the test as working with it.

While trying to answer the questions on the test, have students briefly note on a sheet of paper any items they feel uncertain or unsure about answering.

When they have worked their way through the test, ask the students to share these uncertainties with the class as a whole, discussing the types of concerns they had.

See if there are any systematic patterns among groups of students as to the kinds of concerns they discuss. For example, do the men in the class tend to have specific uncertainties about particular items more often than the women?

How would you and the class assess the importance of these uncertainties in making use of the test results?

Teaching Note

The teacher may choose to structure this activity somewhat by giving students categories that help them both identify and legitimate their thoughts and feelings in responding to test items. For example, students might find that an item is contradictory, or one to which they could respond both "yes" and "no" (or in the case of forced choice items they could strongly prefer or not prefer each item). Additionally, students might find that an item is contingent, that is, their answer would depend on the specific conditions and people involved in the activity asked about by the test. Furthermore, students might find items that seem nonsensical; they do not represent any reality the students know of and therefore they find it difficult to answer.

Asking students to use such categories to classify the items they are uncertain about may in some cases be needed when students are reluctant to criticize a printed, "scientific" test. It should also be noted that prior to doing this activity in class, the teacher should do the test him or herself, noting the uncertainties he or she feels about the specific items.

When possible, ask students to take two or three different tests and compare the similarities and differences in the test results. This is an important way of demonstrating that different tests based on different assumptions can produce different results. Students will come to understand that no one test can "tell the whole truth" about them.

This comparison is best done with tests that have very different assumptions about how the occupational world might or should evolve. For example, there are tests based on the assumption that the occupations in which men and women will experience the greatest degree of satisfaction are those consistent with the sex-role conceptions that students learn early in their lives. These include tests such as Self-Directed Search (SDS), Strong-Campbell Interest Inventory (SCII), the Career Assessment Inventory (CAI), and the Canadian Occupational Interest Inventory (COII). Other tests assume that people will find satisfaction in a wide range of occupations when choice options broaden and non-traditional career opportunities increase. These include tests like the Vocational Interest Experience and Skill Assessment (VIESA).

Many vocational tests are indexed to occupational classification dictionaries (e.g., in Canada the CCDO, or Canadian Classification and Dictionary of Occupations, and in the United States the DOT, or Dictionary of Occupational Titles) so that students can quickly see how well their profiles of interest, aptitudes, and temperaments compare with the standardized descriptions of what characteristics are required to "fit" into a particular occupation. The logic to integrating the structure of test results with the CCDO descriptions runs as follows: First, I find out what I'm like. Then I find out which occupations match this picture of me, and finally, I choose the occupation that best fits who I am. This is the most common "rational decision-making method" advocated by people who create programs of career planning.

Ask students to assess the degree to which people follow a systematic, rational procedure in choosing their jobs or careers by having the class conduct a survey on how people choose their occupations. Students should interview one or two of the employees in their co-op workplaces to obtain information about how those employees chose their particular line of work. The class then compiles this information so that all members of the class can consider the survey results. Together consider such questions as:

- What factors influenced their choices?
- Were the choices largely a result of rational planning and deliberation or a result of circumstances and luck?
- Would a more systematic approach to career planning have been of any use to the people surveyed?
- How were their decisions affected by things that happened outside their life at work?

Here are some hints on how to structure such a survey. Students might begin each interview with the questions: Can you tell me how you came to be working as a _____ here at _____ ? What did you decide to do when you first left high school? As students listen to the person, they should try to write down:

- The critical decision points in the person's life, such as leaving school, getting married, moving.
- The kinds of decisions they had to make, such as choosing a school in which to take training, choosing a job, choosing to stay at home for a while.

- What seemed most important to them at the time they made each of their decisions, for example, security, freedom, love, money, or adventure.
- The approximate order in which they made their decisions.
- How their decisions were related to one another, for example, how the decision to leave school affected their choice of job.

In addition, students should make sure to find out:

- What alternatives were available to the person at the time she or he made each career decision?
- Does the person feel that she or he made a good choice (or series of choices)?
- Is there anything that she or he would do differently if able to make any of the crucial decisions over again?

Activity Three: Using Journal Writing for Self-Assessment

To enhance the educational potential of work experience programs, we need to develop methods whereby students can examine their own experiences and develop an understanding of what experience teaches. To this end student journals are an important and valuable resource. It is therefore recommended that early in the course students begin to keep journals of their work experiences. Journals that will be useful in students' self-assessments should be clearly distinguished from logs or records, which simply describe daily work activities. Indeed, journals are more like diaries. The following activities suggest ways of using student journals in the classroom.

What to Do in the Classroom

Periodically, approximately every two or three weeks, the teacher should ask students to spend some time at home reviewing their journals and marking the entry which: (1) represents a good day at work, one that made them feel good about being there; and (2) represents a bad day at work, one that made them feel that they should have stayed home that morning. This is best done at home so that students have time to read and reflect on their journals. This itself is an important use of journals as students will begin to notice patterns in their experiences which can be discussed and reflected on when they come to class. The teacher makes two lists on the board: "good days" and "bad days." The teacher then asks students to share with the class the journal entries for the days they've marked. The teacher can make clear at the beginning of this exercise that students will be asked to share their experiences so that no student is forced to read an entry she or he does not want heard by others. As the entries are read, the teacher should summarize the characteristics of each entry on the board, gradually building up a list of features that make up good and bad days. After students have read their entries, a class discussion might consider:

1. What features of a good or bad day were commonly experienced?

2. Did students disagree over how they felt about particular features? For example, do students disagree about whether they would characterize "routine" as an aspect of a good or bad day?

3. Did something that was considered part of a good day early in the placement eventually become part of a bad day (or visa versa)?

4. What reasons can students give about why the specific features of a day made them feel it was a good day or a bad day for them?

As an alternative to classifying entries as good days or bad days, the teacher might ask students to classify and discuss entries based on the following distinctions:

• a day when the student felt capable, competent, and had a sense of accomplishment as opposed to a day that he or she felt awkward, incompetent, and incapable of doing things right,

• a day that was really interesting. The student felt involved in what she or he was doing or interested in what was going on at work as opposed to a day that she or he was bored, when there was little happening of any interest.

Toward the end of the students' work placements these entries and discussions might be used to have students write their own self-assessments based on their work experience. Ask them to consider, based on their working experience, what types of work, social conditions, physical environment, and so on would be most desirable to them. Ask for their own assessments of the opportunities they have and the constraints they face in finding work that has such characteristics. Students might together consider how opportunities can be taken advantage of and constraints overcome. The teacher here might encourage the importance of collective problem-solving and support in helping students to define their work in the world.

Activity Four: Other Voices—What Can be Learned from Others' Views of Their Work?

Sometimes students can use what other people say about themselves and the work that they do as a source for self-assessment. Published collections of interviews with working people can be very useful in this regard. Many versions of such publications are widely available in North America—one example would be Studs Terkel's well-known *Working* (New York: Avon Books, 1972), which presents interviews with more than 100 people who talk about what they do all day and how they feel about what they do. What follows are two activities designed to help students reflect on what can be learned from others' views of their work.

What to Do in the Classroom

Choose three or four interviews from a publication such as *Working* that can serve as a rich source of reflection on the relationship between the work that people do and their sense of who they are. Many of the interviews in *Working*, for example, while short enough to read in class, have sufficient interest to be assigned for reading at home.

When students have read a given interview, ask them to think about how the speakers talk and feel about themselves and the work they do. Typically, such interviews present in detail people's understanding of who they are, both as workers and as people. This includes their hopes and dreams, as well as their fears and frustrations. In considering such statements students may clarify some of their own thoughts and feelings about themselves and their futures at work. Below are a number of suggested activities oriented to this purpose.

1. Have students write or role play a conversation between two people from *Working* (or similar publication) in which both find out what thoughts and feelings about their jobs they have in common and in what ways they differ.

2. Role play a TV panel show, asking each of four students to act as one of the people interviewed in the collection chosen for discussion.

3. Ask students if there is anyone at their workplace (or where they may hold part-time jobs) that reminds them of any of the people they have read about. Have them write a brief statement about ways in which they are similar. Alternatively, if they cannot think of anyone, ask them to identify someone who holds the opposite view of their work to one of the people they have read about. Have them write a brief statement of the ways in which the two people differ.

Another way of helping students to clarify their thoughts and feelings about work experience is by asking them to talk to one or two employees at their workplace. Have students, if possible, get a sense of how people feel about their work, and why or why not it is important to them. The objective is to give students more perspective on their own experiences through comparisons with what other people say and feel about what they do at the workplace.

Once students have done one or two interviews, have them share both what they have learned and their interviewing experiences in class. Encourage them to talk about how they felt, what problems they had (if any), and if there were any questions they wanted to ask but felt they couldn't.

It might be possible in some cases to have students publish their interviews as a collection of views that different people have about work. In such a publication the students' views of their own work and their thoughts on what other people say about work should be included. The sense of an "end product" that will be distributed to and read by others can give students the experience of being involved in a useful, productive endeavor. It will also give students the sense that their thoughts and feelings count and deserve to be heard, and the knowledge that working collectively can be a source of accomplishment, pride, and fun.

Activity Five: Job Descriptions—Is This Job Right for You?

Self-assessment is commonly understood as a way of answering questions such as: Am I right for this job? Does this career suit me? Can I do this type of work? In determining whether a particular job or type of work is appropriate, the usual procedure is to compare some personal characteristics (e.g., interests, temperaments, aptitudes, etc.) against some set of job requirements. This means that jobs must be "objectively" described and defined and that such job descriptions become the standard against which people are counselled, hired, paid, and evaluated.

Those involved in work experience programs often take for granted that through working, students will learn enough about particular types of work to determine whether or not they want to pursue such occupations in the future. In the workplace it is assumed that they can get the kind of firsthand knowledge of job requirements that will enable them to assess whether or not such work is right for them. Teachers often comment that "work experience gives the kids a chance to find out if they are cut out for this or that kind of work."

There is, however, a problem in all this. What is often forgotten is that job requirements are not fixed but rather are dependent on a range of decisions made by employers or managers as to how a set of tasks will be defined and related to each other. Organizations can and do differ in how the work they require is assigned and distributed among its members. Such decisions are based not only on the nature of the work itself but also on the values held with regard to how work should be organized, the importance of hierarchy, the question of supervision, and economic pressures the organization might face.

What is the importance of this for self-assessment? It means that teachers should attempt to help students understand that their reactions to particular work experiences are reactions to other people's plans and ideas for how a particular type of job should be done. Thus, self-assessment using work experience is not finding out about yourself (in terms of essential characteristics) but rather finding out about your interest in and ability to fit *one version* of the existing reality of work. This also means that students can be challenged to find out if there are alternative versions of what certain jobs entail within specific occupational areas. Further, they may wish to assess what ways of organizing work and defining jobs would be most desirable for them. From this vantage point a range of questions can be posed:

- How much variety in how work gets done exists among organizations?
- Why do you suppose this is the case?
- If you don't fit in with the way work you want to do is most often defined, what are the consequences?
- Are there any options?

Below you will find several activities that will help students understand that jobs are not independent from the people who do them and the organizations that define them. These activities ask students to investigate the way jobs are defined in their own placements.

What to Do in the Classroom

As indicated in Chapter 4, job descriptions often attempt to specify the knowledge, skills, and abilities required to do a particular job. Job descriptions differ from each other not only in terms of these requirements but also in the number, variety, and level of complexity of items specified in a description. Therefore jobs (more precisely, job descriptions) can be compared in terms of the opportunities they provide for people to exercise their knowledge, skills, and abilities and the scope that they provide for the development and extension of the capabilities people bring to their work.

After students have been at their workplace for several weeks, ask them to write up job descriptions for themselves based on what they have been doing. Suggested categories for these descriptions are:

- what I need to know about
- what I need to know how to do
- what tasks I perform
- what I am responsible for

Have students find out if the organizations they are placed in have official written job descriptions. If not, see if they can find out why not. If so, have them obtain or copy the official descriptions for their own jobs. Each student who is able to do this may then compare his or her own version of the job with the official one. Have students note any differences and share them with the class. Ask the class to suggest why such differences might exist.

Ask students to write a job description for one of the employees they work with based on what they have observed that person doing and discussions they have had with the person. Then the students might:

- share this description with the person, asking him or her to suggest any changes that should be made to make the description more accurate. Students should consider why they might not have been aware of particular aspects of the job.
- obtain or copy the official job description for that position and compare their version with the official one. Ask students to note any differences and share these with the class.

Assuming that the teacher has access to and a passing familiarity with the *Canadian Classification and Dictionary of Occupations* (CCDO) or the *Dictionary of Occupational Titles* (DOT), help students to locate their own jobs and the job of at least one of the employees they work with in the dictionary. Note any differences between the way students describe these jobs and how they are described in this occupational index. Discuss with the class why such differences might exist.

Have students interview at least one person who is doing a job similar to their own but in a different workplace. Students should bring the job descriptions they have written to the interview. The purpose of the interview is to ask whether or not the description written by the student accurately reflects the work done by the person being interviewed. Students should ask what additions and deletions should be made to modify the description to fit the work done by this person. They should discuss reasons for any differences they have identified. This activity is most valuable if students can find people to interview who work in organizations that differ from their placements in such characteristics as size of organization, employment sector, or mode of production.

11

Speaking Out about Pay

This guy across the street, he's only got grade nine education, you know, and he's working at a hospital—maintenance, you know. Put it this way, there's a lot of people I know that have no education but they're out there making money. Like, he's making good money, right?

(Anthony)

As a topic for discussion or focus of inquiry, pay is almost always excluded from work-education programs. The most common justifications for what we take to be a rather glaring omission are: (1) that pay is private, a personal matter, and to ask questions about it would be "nosy" and inappropriate; and (2) that for students, especially "lower-level" students who are presumed to be headed for lower-level jobs, talk of pay only adds insult to injury. They already know that the jobs they will get are low paying and to point it out to them only makes them feel bad, unimportant, and/or worthless. This chapter is based on a different set of assumptions: that the secrecy surrounding pay always disadvantages the poorly paid; and that the presumed relation between pay and worth ignores questions of power in determining who gets paid how much to do what. If part of the point of a critical pedagogy of work education is to include issues of social and economic justice into the ordinarily innocuous work-education curriculum, then the topic of pay must be taken up and dealt with directly in class.

Understanding paid employment as an exchange relation and being knowledgeable about wages and salaries are important for students both as workers and as citizens. As workers, they will have to make regular decisions on the basis of what they understand to be fair pay: Should I take this job at this rate of pay? What kinds of increases should we demand in our next round of negotiations? If I need childcare to work, how much should I pay for it? As citizens, they will have to come to conclusions about whether to support or oppose a regressive tax proposal, to cross a picket line, to participate in a boycott, based in part on their understanding of how people get paid, how much they get paid, and what is fair.

Many students will come into the classroom already knowing quite a bit about pay. The most direct source of their knowledge about the wage-labor exchange will likely have been their own part-time and summer jobs. Although clearly a good place to start an exploration of pay, the experience of part-time work has its limitations. This work is characteristically unskilled, casual, and paid at minimum wage. The relative ease with which many students move into and out of this youth labor market produces a common perception of frequent and unproblematic job turnover. Many students note the ease with which jobs are found, done for a while, then left. In addition, students typically make minimal claims on the jobs they hold and are often swayed by what appear to be better jobs, usually for reasons of pay increases, but also because of other benefits (staff discounts on merchandise, closeness to home, better hours). Dissatisfaction with jobs in the youth labor market is most easily and often solved by quitting rather than taking complaints to management. While such a strategy might be sufficient for dealing with problems in part-time, casual employment, job-hopping is less likely to be an effective strategy for dealing with problems, difficulties, and dissatisfactions in full-time, regular work. This chapter is intended therefore to extend the understandings of pay students already have to include a consideration of such questions as: What are they, as workers, exchanging for a wage? What are the kinds of claims bosses and supervisors can make on them because of what they get paid? What is fair pay?

Another source of knowledge about the wage labor exchange is students' familiarity with parents' and other family members' work and work histories. Many students will have experienced situations of parental lay-off or unemployment. They might also have a quite sophisticated understanding of fluctuations in type, intensity, and duration of work, plant closure, and relocation. The classroom then provides the opportunity for students to work with the experiences of others to explore their own understandings of the wage-labor exchange. What perceptions do they have, for example, of what their parents are exchanging for a wage? How do they understand relations of exchange as shaping their own family lives, and also possibilities and desires for the future?

What do students see as fair or unfair in their parents' relation to jobs and to structures of pay? In other words, part of what we want to explore in this chapter are those factors students already know when they come into the classroom and those decisions they might already have made about their own futures.

Additionally, students will have some familiarity with divisions of labor (although not naming them as such) along class and gender lines. Many will come to the classroom with received ideas about "professionals" and "workers" in relation to pay and income. Many will hold conventional beliefs about work options for women and men. Some will see divisions in the labor force along lines of gender, class, race and ethnicity, age, and ability/disability as "natural" and just. It is precisely this kind of commonsense understanding that this chapter is designed to address. While acknowledging that students come to the classroom (and the workplace) already knowing some things about pay, the activities suggested here encourage students to broaden the base of their knowledge by gathering information from want ads, friends, relatives, co-workers, and strangers, and then challenging them to think critically about the issue of pay in relation to their own working lives and the working lives of others. We want to encourage them to ask questions about the limitations and possibilities of existing structures of exchange relations. And we want them to consider what kinds of changes would be required to make fairness the basis of the exchange.

This chapter is divided into the following sections:

• Activity One: Ways of getting paid: piecework, wages, and salaries
• Activity Two: Good money
• Activity Three: Who benefits?
• Activity Four: What's fair?
• Activity Five: Pay equity

Activity One: Ways of Getting Paid: Piecework, Wages, and Salaries

Different people get paid differently. This is true not only in terms of the amount of payment but also in terms of the way that amount is established. While ways of getting paid are neither given nor fixed, there is a fair degree of commonality among kinds of jobs in determining how people will be paid. Plumbers are usually paid by the hour. Sales representatives often work on commission. Consultants are sometimes paid so much per day plus expenses. These ways of getting paid are not just conventional—that is, "the way it has always been done." They are based on certain assumptions about self-interest, control, responsibility, and productivity, which this activity is designed to explore.

What to Do in the Classroom

The teacher should introduce three basic ways of getting paid: piecework or commission, hourly wage, and salary (bearing in mind that there are combinations and variations of these three basic means, such as quota plus bonus, minimum wage plus tips, time and materials, etc.). Using these means as headings on the board, have the class generate a list of occupations that typify the various ways of getting paid. When a suitable range of occupations has been suggested, a partial list might look something like this:

Piecework/commission	Hourly wage	Salary
garment worker	cashier	teacher
dentist	plumber	manager
fruit picker	postal worker	executive
artist	musician	fire fighter

Organize a discussion of the various ways of getting paid with the following kinds of questions:

- What are the advantages or disadvantages of being paid by the piece? By the hour? By the year? For the employee? For the employer?
- Does one means clearly advantage either the employer or the employee?
- Would it be possible or desirable to pay everyone using the same means? Why? Why not?

  For example, would it be possible to pay a farm worker a salary? Would it be desirable? Would it be possible to pay a teacher an hourly wage? Would it be desirable? Would be it possible to pay a postal worker by the piece? Would it be desirable?

Teaching Note

The point of this discussion is to make explicit some of the underlying assumptions of each of the ways of getting paid. Focusing on the issues of self-interest, control, responsibility and productivity, essential differences in means should become apparent. For example, in piecework, because pay is directly linked to production, counting schemes and mechanisms are emphasized over direct supervision. Hourly wages are usually paid when there is no such direct link to production and so supervision of employees is seen to be more important.

Activity Two: Good Money

In everyday talk it is not uncommon to hear that someone or some group of people is making "pretty good money." While there is no precise definition of what exactly "good money" is, one common way of understanding it is that good money refers to a match between one's income and one's financial needs. But people's financial needs differ and so, therefore, does their conception of what constitutes good money. What are considered to be financial needs are also influenced by desires within the contexts of life circumstances. To a person living with parents accustomed to working part-time for minimum wage, a summer job that pays $10 per hour sounds like pretty good money. To a sole-support parent of two school-age children, the same wage would be less than adequate. There is also a sense, however, in which good money refers to earnings relative to other peoples' incomes. It is in this sense that we can say that someone (or some group) makes good money regardless of their financial obligations. From this perspective, anyone who makes $100,000 per year is making good money whether or not they are able to pay their bills. The following activity is designed to encourage an exploration into both aspects of the notion of good money.

What to Do in the Classroom

The first part of this activity is to create a table that establishes equivalence between wages and salaries. A sample of such a table is provided below:

Dollars per

hour	day	week	month	year
5	40	200	800	7,200
10	80	400	1600	14,400
50	400	2000	8000	72,000

(This table is based on an eight-hour day and a 40-hour week.)

Students can complete the table individually, in small groups, or as a class. The table itself can be filled out from both directions, starting from an hourly wage and working toward an annual income, or starting from an annual salary and working toward an hourly rate. For example, the teacher might begin by asking, "If a person makes $5 per hour, how much does she or her make per week and per year?" Conversely, the teacher could ask, "If someone makes $100,000 per year, how much does she or he make per day?"

Have students research the rates and modes of pay for different jobs of particular interest to them. Using personal contacts, career development materials, want ads, and other sources of information on wages and salaries, have students plot on the table the wage and salary data they have collected, including the jobs to which the information applies.

Have the students consider and discuss the results of their research. How do they understand and/or explain the degree of difference in pay provided people in this society? Which of these differences are seen as fair or unfair? What degree of difference is necessary or tolerable?

Teaching Note

Due to the fact that the above table is based on an eight-hour day and a 40-hour week, there is a certain amount of distortion in this exercise which should be pointed out if students themselves don't raise the issue. Someone who makes $25 per hour might or might not work eight hours per day. Someone who charges $1000 per day plus expenses might spend four days a week looking for work. Seasonal employment is not taken into account. It is difficult to calculate hours per day for some kinds of work (like teaching).

Activity Three: Who Benefits?

In addition to wages per se, some employees receive additional kinds of compensation for their work, which are ordinarily referred to as benefits. Such benefits might range from a complimentary pair of safety glasses worth $14.95 to stock options worth thousands of dollars. The following activity is intended to familiarize students with the wide range of perks, payments, and privileges that go under the rubric of benefits, and to examine the distribution of benefits in the work force.

What to Do in the Classroom

On the blackboard or chart paper list all the benefits students have received, heard about, and/or imagined. The list might include:

health insurance	safety shoes	vacations
sick days	parking	lunch/dinner
expense account	dental care	parental leave
childcare	stock options	room and board
pension plan	company car	discounts

Drawing on the combined knowledge of the class, discuss the distribution of benefits across different categories of workers. Which of these benefits are enjoyed by all employees? Which apply only to wage earners and which to salaried employees? Which apply mainly to men and which to women? Students can then begin to discuss the assumptions behind these distributions.

Activity Four: What's Fair?

What do we exchange in the exchange relation? What is the employer buying? Our time? Our labor? Our knowledge and skills? Or ourselves? How students understand and answer this question has important implications for how they establish themselves in the workplace and the extent to which they are able to exert control over the practices which determine their working lives. In other words, how they understand the terms of the exchange is fundamental to understanding that there might be a difference between who they are and who they are supposed to be at work, and between what they might think is the appropriate thing to do and what they are expected to do because they're "on the employers' time."

It is not uncommon in work-study program for students to take exception to being assigned routine, monotonous, low-level tasks. The early-childhood student resents being assigned to do materials preparation. The automotive student doesn't see the point of his being required to change tires day after day. The hospitality and recreation student is disappointed that she spends so much time answering the phone. Hairdressing students sweep floors. Baking students crack eggs. Drafting students copy drawings. Auto body students sand and sand and sand. Are these students being exploited or is it "just part of the job?" When the employer buys time or labor (with wages or the opportunity to earn course credits) what is fair for the employer to expect? In trying to determine what's fair in any particular instance, it's important to establish the sense in which the employer and the employee understand the terms of the exchange. For example:

1. Is the exchange based on an a priori specification of tasks? In other words, is the person being paid to do a particular job (and only that job)? If the dishwasher is paid to work in the kitchen, is it fair to ask her or him to cut the grass or wash the windows?

2. Is the exchange based on the application of particular skills or knowledges? If the office worker is paid to type, can she or he be selective about what is typed? Should she or he be expected to make coffee?

3. Is the exchange based on the unspecified use of labor power (constrained only by societal norms and/or the law)? If the worker is paid to do what she or he is told to do on company time, is there anything that could be considered unfair?

Teaching Note

This activity focuses on the question of fairness in the exchange relation. It should also be recognized, however, that exchange is only one feature of the social relations in which people participate at work. What might not seem fair in terms of the exchange could possibly be understood and/or justified with reference to another feature of social relations—for example, "It might not be fair but I'm doing it as a favor or because I don't really mind doing it."

What to Do in the Classroom

The following partial transcript can be used to introduce the issue of fairness in the exchange. Guided by the questions outlined above, students should be prepared to critique and discuss Mick's position on fairness with reference to their own understandings of what is bought and sold in the exchange relations in which they currently participate.

He wanted me to paint the place, right. We made a contract and he broke the contract! And I got mad and so I didn't finish painting his place . . . and now he took a fit about it. We had a deal. Seventy-five dollars for four hours, right. And it took me eight hours so I wanted $150. And he didn't pay me, not even the $75! He paid me $50 for eight hours work. . . . He owes me, paying me by the hour, right.

Mick

After discussing Mick's case as a class, break into small groups to explore the issue of fairness in the exchange relative to current workplace. Within each group, decide on one particularly interesting case. Choose two members of the group each willing to argue opposite sides of the fairness question. Establish a "fairness tribunal" made up of five to seven students charged with determining the fairness or unfairness of the cases brought before it. Have each group present its case to the tribunal for a ruling.

Teaching Note

A separate issue, but one related to the question of what's fair, is the question of what's right. While employers might (or might not) reasonably require employees to do things they would rather not do on the basis of it being the "employers time," there are certainly some circumstances in which the employee can reasonably refuse to do assigned work (where issues of health and safety are concerned, for example). The question here is: Are there other circumstances in which a person's integrity might be compromised such that it warrants a refusal? The range of circumstances that might be considered here range from the near trivial to the outright criminal (e.g., covering for the boss on the phone, "She's not here right now, can I take a message?" or falsifying receipts, compulsory socializing, unscrupulous sales tactics, pilfering materials, etc.).

Activity Five: Pay Equity

In a culture where men weave and women fish, just as in a culture where men fish and women weave, . . . whichever activity is assigned to the male is the activity with the greater prestige, power, status, and rewards.

Margaret Mead

In Ontario, on average, there is a 35 percent difference between wages and salaries paid to men and women. This difference is called the "wage gap." This gap between the compensation and recognition afforded men and women for what they do is, as Margaret Mead points out, nothing new. Historically, those kinds of activities that are regarded as women's work will not be valued or paid as highly as those activities that are regarded as men's work. In industrial societies, wages and salaries earned by women have been related less to the actual work performed and more on assumptions that women are normally "dependents," working only for "pin money," and/or that women are naturally subordinate.

Initial efforts by women's groups and trade unions to close this wage gap centered on demands for equal pay for equal work. This strategy was intended to remedy the most blatant forms of wage discrimination by ensuring that employees performing the same (or similar) work receive the same pay, regardless of gender.

The problem with this initial approach was that it didn't take into account the gendered/gendering features of the overall division of labor—that is, that men and women tend to do different jobs. "Equal pay for equal work" didn't provide for comparisons between dissimilar jobs to determine relative worth. That Ontario nurses make 44 percent of what Ontario engineers make, for example, or that childcare workers make 47 percent of industrial workers' wages are inequities that remain unaddressable because the work itself is said to be incomparable.

Recognition of the systemic wage discrimination against women who work in predominantly "female occupations" or job classes has led to a revised strategy for closing the gap between men's and women's wages. Pay equity, as a strategy, is founded on the principle that work usually done by women must be compared to that usually done by men to ensure equal pay for work of equal value.

A pay equity plan requires at least two things: a description of all the work to be studied; and an evaluation schema to define/measure the value of the work.

There are many "plans" for assessing job value. Most rely on a factor analysis comprised of at least four categories, which often include:

- skill—training and experience required
- effort (sometimes called mental demands)—judgment and problem-solving abilities
- accountability—responsibility for making decisions
- working conditions—physical effort, or exposure to hazardous conditions

What to Do in the Classroom

With the class, develop a ten-point scale for each of the above factors. For example, in terms of accountability, the number one might represent "no responsibility"; five might represent "responsible for routine decision-making"; and ten might represent "sole responsibility for major decisions."

Using these criteria developed in class, have each student evaluate one or more jobs at her or his workplace. Use these data to compare several jobs. For example, the class might compare the job of childcare worker with that of draftsperson. They might conclude that while the draftsperson requires more effort and enjoys better working conditions than the childcare worker, the job of caring for children requires more responsibility, physical effort, and skill. In this case, the overall value of the childcare worker could be the same or greater than that of the draftsperson. The childcare worker, then, should be paid the same amount or more than the draftsperson. Ask the class to ascertain whether or not this is in fact the case. Compare several jobs this way, paying particular attention to comparisons of male-dominated and female-dominated occupations.

Some critics have charged that pay equity is a technical solution to a political problem. They argue that the injustice of wage discrimination and the problem of getting money into the hands of women who need and deserve it remain largely unaffected by pay equity programs. They suggest that energies spent doing job comparisons might be better directed at efforts to increase minimum wages, to organize workers in female occupations, and to support job actions for better wages. Invite a pay equity advocate and a pay equity critic to your class to debate this issue.

12

Getting a Job

For many high school and college students, getting a job is not a new experience. Important insights have been won in the context of their struggles to find jobs and keep them. These insights, however, most often exist as fragments, as an unconnected set of ideas that revolve around the notion of "selling yourself" as the most important principle in the process of getting a job. This chapter is an attempt to broaden such commonsense understandings by considering the process of getting a job as an exchange relation. This perspective on the job acquisition process can help students establish a presence in the hiring situation that will allow them to more effectively negotiate the terms of the exchange without ceding the situation entirely to employer prerogative.

The following activities are contained in this chapter:

- Activity One: Resumes and the wage-labor exchange
- Activity Two: The politics of the job interview
- Activity Three: What can they ask about me?
- Activity Four: It's whom you know
- Activity Five: Recognizing differences in job-search strategies

Activity One: Resumes and the Wage-Labor Exchange

"It's like selling your house," said one student, "you describe all the good points first." Another said, "You just tell your good points. You want to be hired, you want money, so you're gonna obviously talk about good points about yourself, what you can do." Someone wondered if that was like packaging yourself. One student said, "That's right— McNuggets." Another added, "I don't see nothing wrong with it, depending on how you do it—as long as you don't lie."

What is the work that resumes do? As the students in the above paragraph recognize, resumes are not representations of the total value of people's experience or capabilities. Rather, resumes are a particular tool for prospective employees to use in conveying information to employers in a manner that might enhance a person's likelihood of obtaining a job. In this sense, resumes are a resource that people can use for accessing and influencing the terms of a wage-labor exchange.

There are several different ways that resumes can be written. Providing students with only a single standardized format can restrict their ability to make sense of what is really a complicated set of questions, problems, and issues. The following suggestions may be useful in raising some of these concerns.

What to Do in the Classroom

Through class discussion, generate a preliminary list of the categories of information resumes might well include. Some categories may seem straightforward, while others may be controversial. For example, is marital status an important category? What about citizenship, sexual orientation, or the last book an applicant read? Is there any disagreement about the appropriateness of particular categories? If so, consider them with the following questions: What are employers interested in knowing about job applicants? What are job applicants interested in telling employers about themselves? How might this vary with the particular job for which one is applying? What kinds of information seem awkward or inappropriate to provide? Who is disadvantaged by the provision of some kinds of information?

Resumes may take several formats. A preliminary distinction can easily be made between chronological and functional resumes.[1] A chronological resume presents an organized overview of major elements in a person's work (and work-related) history. A functional resume focuses attention on particular kinds of work-related skills and clarifies their relevance for a specific job. Because of its relative simplicity, often only chronological resumes are taught, yet functional resumes have much to recommend them. The opportunity for students to prepare both chronological and functional resumes and then to compare the two provides an occasion for thinking analytically about the role of resumes in the job-search process.

Hand out samples of both kinds of resumes and ask the class to answer the questions: Which is easier (or more difficult) to follow, and why?

Which more (or less) successfully presents personal capabilities and related experiences, and why? Which seems easier (or more difficult) to
construct, and why?

While chronological and functional resumes have standard currency
in the world of work, they are not the only ways that students can
present information about themselves. Through class participation, generate several alternative formats that vary from the traditional models.
Students might imagine how to vary categories, order of presentation
on the page, and document length. They may consider whether to include pictures, multi-colored print, "scratch and sniff" features, and so
on. Within basic limits, individuals should be encouraged to experiment
with different ways of presenting information taking into account who
they are and what kinds of jobs they are looking for. Explore with the
class the assumptions students have made about why a particular format
may be effective.

Clearly, students will want to put the best representation of themselves in their resumes. However, there are questions about where to
draw the line between a positive presentation and an outright distortion.
If a student regularly babysits for brothers and sisters in the home, is
the claim that one has experience working with children warranted? Is
the facility for using a single word-processing program grounds for making the claim to computer competence? Furthermore, there are questions
of the degree of omission allowed in writing the resume. For example,
if one is 18 years old and has only partial high school credit, should
information as to academic achievement be omitted? Should periods of
unemployment simply be omitted? If such questions have not arisen
during the discussion of resume writing it will be important to raise
them with the class.

Activity Two: The Politics of the Job Interview

A common practice for preparing students for job interviews is to
emphasize lists of do's and don'ts. There is no lack of sources of advice
on how to be a good interviewee. Our view is not that lists of do's and
don'ts have no value for teaching and learning about job interviews in
work education. Rather, in our view they need to be incorporated into
a perspective on the dynamics of the wage-labor exchange and the structure of power inherent in the job interview situation. Interviews need
to be understood as events that interviewees can themselves influence
in various ways. Interviews are not just something that happens to the
interviewee, totally under the interviewer's control. In this regard, learning about interviews involves paying attention to both sides of the relationship and seeing it as an interactive process.

What to Do in the Classroom

There are many films and videotapes widely available that portray the
dynamics of job interviews. The best are constructed in an open-ended

fashion in which several applicants are interviewed and the one who is hired is not disclosed. Beyond a discussion of "who would you hire?" we recommend a more focused viewing. The following are some suggestions.

1. Very often the first four or five minutes of a job interview are crucial for setting the tone for the remainder of the interview. Each applicant in the film or video can be assessed and compared by the class for just that segment of the interview.

2. Different students can be assigned to pay particular attention to different aspects of the interview: posture, gestures, interest and involvement, spoken language, references to past experiences, difficult questions, strengths and weaknesses, and so on. Various observations and insights could be consolidated.

3. For students to develop a more complete understanding of the job interview situation, they need to consider the interviewer's role in the process. What is the interviewer trying to accomplish? How good a job does she or he do in the interview? What interviewing strategies are being used? Does she or he act differently when interviewing different applicants? What seems to please or displease the interviewer (and how do you know this)? What are the implications of the answers to these questions for how interviewees need to act in the interview situation?

4. Do there seem to be key turning points (positive or negative) in the interview? If so, how were they produced in interaction between interviewee and interviewer? If things were going poorly, what might the interviewee have done to turn things around?

Role playing job interviews is a valuable and commonly used technique in work-study courses. It can give students a chance to practice specific behaviors considered by many interviewers to be important (e.g., maintaining eye-contact, asking questions about the job); it can help them practice answers to questions they can expect to be asked (e.g., about related experience, successes, and problems at school); it can alert them to mannerisms they may want to control (e.g., slouching, starting sentences with "Like"); and in general it can assist them to approach an interview more relaxed and with greater confidence.

It may be useful to continue the use of role playing throughout the course, and even to vary its format. A single practice session is not likely to accomplish very substantial learning, especially for behavior in a situation as complex as a job interview. In addition, the more occasions students have to view each other's role-play interviews, and to compare and assess the techniques they see each other using, the greater the likelihood that everyone will benefit. There are a few points to consider when planning role-play interviews.

1. In order to introduce students to the variety of interviewer styles that exist, different interviewers should be used in role playing whenever possible.

2. Interview segments are one useful way to approach the exercise. For example, the opening few minutes can be repeated several times. Or a difficult question can be repeated until the student is happy with the answer.

3. The interviewer can be asked to role play a specific attitude or disposition, thus providing the student with the added challenge of "reading" the situation and devising a strategy in action. For example, if the interviewer assumes an attitude related to a recent negative experience with a work-study student, he or she might appear reluctant to accept another. Another orientation that the role-play interviewer might adopt is one of being overworked and having insufficient time for the interview.

4. If videotaping is used, several variations might be considered. Camera angle is one possibility: Filming over the interviewer's shoulder gives one perspective, and over the interviewee's, another. During playback, if either the audio or the video is used alone, different kinds of information are highlighted for assessment. If students were taped at the start of the course, they might be retaped toward the end so that learning could be demonstrated, and areas for additional improvement suggested.

Activity Three: What Can They Ask about Me?

Students need to know their lawful rights in the context of negotiating the wage-labor exchange, particularly their right not to suffer discrimination during interviews and in filling out application forms. Most questions asked by employers are appropriate to the screening process. Some questions, however, have either the purpose or the effect of illegally preventing people from obtaining jobs they would be well able to do.

Students need to be able to recognize discriminatory practices during the job interview. They need to have some useful ideas for what to do (and how to think through the situation) when they sense their legal rights are being jeopardized. From the job-seeker's perspective, discrimination in hiring is seldom blatant and direct. Neither is it pleasant to dwell on. These factors can easily discourage students from naming the experience of discrimination and claiming that in fact an act of injustice has occurred.

Teachers are often hesitant to believe and reluctant to support a student's claim. Many work-education programs stress the importance of satisfying employer expectations. Some teachers may feel that teaching students to assert their legal rights against possible discrimination in hiring would seem to rub against the grain of intentions of the program within which they are teaching. Despite all the complexity and risk, not to address legal protections in the job search is to avoid what we believe to be a primary goal of work education: to increase their effective participation in determining the practices that define their working lives.

Because of the common notion that discrimination is always intentional and always based directly on personal prejudice, people often fail to notice ways in which institutional arrangements and procedures routinely disadvantage certain people in favor of others. For example, young job applicants' typical lack of familiarity with legal rights and lack of access to legal remedies in the hiring process is a kind of institutional guarantee that discrimination will go unacknowledged, unchallenged, and unchanged at the point of first entry into the labor force. When schools fail to inform students of legal protections, they become (albeit unintentionally) participants in institutional discrimination.

What to Do in the Classroom

While the learning needs are clear, the challenge of meeting them is far more complex. Knowing the details of relevant laws (and their respective jurisdictions and remedies) is difficult for many teachers themselves to accomplish. We recommend that the task of gathering information concerning fair employment practices be seen as the responsibility of the class as a whole.

Human rights codes are key texts because they establish the official protection of law against discrimination in hiring. Students should get a chance to actually see the code relevant to the jurisdiction in which they live. The purpose of collectively examining such a code is to make cautious entry into its language and content—not to pretend to expertise, but rather to gain confidence and familiarity with its existence and to get a concrete appreciation of its potential for their lives. Key sections (regarding definitions, coverage, and enforcement) should be highlighted. One good way to do this is to ask the class, in small groups, to search available codes to find all the sections that say anything relevant to discrimination in employment. When attending to the matter of enforcement, be sure to clarify jurisdictional differences between local, provincial, and federal laws.

Formally filing claims of discrimination under the law can be a troubling and time-consuming experience. Students therefore need information about the variety of supports that exist in the community to help claimants. Assign each small group the task of locating offices, agencies, and individuals in the community that are available to help job-seekers combat apparent discrimination in hiring. If possible, schedule time for the groups to visit these places and people so that they can get a more personal and detailed sense of what is involved, or invite outside experts to address the class, perhaps in a panel format.

Teaching Note

In some cases teachers may find that they have a student in their class who seems to have a legitimate complaint in relation to job-hiring discrimination. This may have occurred in the context of a student's attempt to find either summer or part-time employment. If this is the case, it would be instructive for the class as a whole to help this student fill out and file an official complaint. This has the advantage of having the class work with the real complexities and issues raised by such events.

Activity Four: It's Whom You Know

Concerning the value of informal networks, grapevines, or contacts in finding jobs, there is unusual agreement between popular opinion and research studies. Informal sources of information, assistance, referral and even hiring are among the most important ingredients—if not the single most important—in securing employment. Why? There are at least two reasons. First, it is cheaper both in terms of time and money because it eliminates advertising costs and reduces time spent on screening applicants. Second, contrary to the rhetoric of selling yourself through resumes or within interviews, many employers are more likely to trust recommendations from friends and their own employees. This is so because neither friends nor employees are likely to recommend people who would compromise their relationship with the employer.

However, networks do not work for everybody. Because networks function through informal social relations, those people excluded or without access to these relations can often be eliminated from being considered for available jobs. Informal networks reproduce forms of institutional discrimination, most notably racism and sexism. Indeed, networks are such powerful means of getting a job that groups who have historically been disadvantaged often use the success of a few in securing employment in areas previously closed to provide access to others.

What follows are some suggestions for teaching about job-search networks and grapevines in work-education programs, and in particular, of the important role informal contacts can play in finding work.

What to Do in the Classroom

Each student selects an occupation and (over time, probably several weeks) puts together a personal grapevine of contacts and sources of useful information and assistance about the chosen occupation. Who's hiring? What are the working conditions, pay, and benefits? What experiences and credentials are necessary or helpful? To what extent is the occupation unionized? How is the field of work changing locally and regionally?

The chosen occupation can be one the student is already somewhat familiar with, or one he or she has no information about. In either case the occupation should relate to work done at the student's workplace in order that the exercise can help sustain the relationship between in-school and workplace learning.

Identify and make at least preliminary contact with a certain (assigned or suggested) number of primary sources—that is, people currently doing the chosen kind of job, or who have done that kind of job, or who are preparing themselves to do that kind of job, or hiring people who do that kind of job, or related to people doing that kind of job. This is the informal network.

Identify and make at least preliminary contact with a certain (assigned or suggested) number of secondary sources of information about the chosen kind of job—that is, employment agencies (public and private), unions or occupational associations, service clubs, libraries, guidance facilities, governmental offices, and so on. This is the formal network.

For purposes of this exercise, what students learn about their chosen job from informal and formal contacts is less important than what they learn about how a job-finding network is actually constructed—the challenges, skills, frustrations, satisfactions, and benefits. To add focus to the exercise, however, the class might well generate a common list of relevant topics or questions for everyone to attempt to answer from the grapevines they are able to construct.

Through discussion and feedback, students should benefit tremendously from each other's experiences with networks: tips on how and where to look, what to say and how to say it, common mistakes and how to avoid them, how to recognize truly useful information, and ways to keep records. Students may also begin to sense how networks function as a form of exclusion and are thus implicated in the reproduction of discriminatory practices.

Obviously, different techniques are required to make primary contacts than to locate useful secondary sources (offices, agencies, groups, etc.). This is an important distinction, and one easy to clarify when based on the actual experiences of the students in the class. Being able to appreciate this distinction and to find useful ways to apply it will help the class define its collective thinking about network-building.

Consideration might well be given to making the "create a grapevine" assignment a small-group task, rather than an individual task. It is easy to presume that job-finding is inevitably an individual process, since the labor market is commonly thought of as a competitive arena. However, there are several good reasons to suggest that job-search effectiveness increases when done collectively, rather than individually. By framing the assignment as a small-group task, the class will be given an experimental basis for reconsidering its understanding of this aspect of job-finding.

Activity Five: Recognizing Differences in Job-Search Strategies

There is no end of "expert" advice about how a job search should be done. However, much of this advice is given in the abstract without taking into account the specific circumstances of job-seekers and local economies. What in fact are the ways that people actually do go about looking for work? What are job searchers' opinions about effective job-search techniques, about the major aids and barriers to finding employment? Taking up these issues will allow the teacher to explore with the class some of the actual conditions students will face in obtaining employment.

What to Do in the Classroom

Survey the class for the job-search strategies used by students in finding part-time or summer employment. For example, have students list all the strategies they have used in trying to find a job and the outcome of using these strategies. The outcomes here refer to the following options: resulted in no job; resulted in minimum-wage job or lower (e.g., babysitting); resulted in better than minimum-wage job.

Organize the data collected into a few simple tables and graphs. Present this material to the class for discussion and interpretation. Is there an apparent connection, for example, between strategy and outcome?

Another way of expanding students' understanding of these data is to compare them with other surveys that have reported on similar questions. The Canadian report *Youth/Jeunesse: A New Statistical Perspective on Youth in Canada* (Hull: Minister of State for Youth, Communications Directorate, undated, early 1980s) is a good illustration of such a survey. For example, one of its data sets (126) concerns job search activities of persons 15–24 years (pp. 304–5). These data allow a comparison of people attending school full time with people not attending school full time. A lesson using these few tables and graphs would allow the following questions to be raised:

- Which are the most frequently used methods (of each group)?

- What are the similarities and differences between job search patterns?

- What accounts for the apparent preference of certain methods over other methods? Where have these preferences probably been learned?

- Which combinations of methods might be most effective?

- How does the information in this data set compare with advice provided by job-search manuals and brochures? What might account for any apparent differences?

NOTE

1. Teachers unfamiliar with these distinctions can find numerous examples in material at guidance offices and employment centers as well as in business education guidelines in many school board jurisdictions.

13

Future Work

We are standing at the foot of a mountain with a technological avalanche about to come down on us. . . . The introduction and speed of the new chip technology can't be stopped because it is the engine of growth and productivity. . . . The next fifteen to twenty years will see a massive restructuring of society as a result of new technology. (*Future Work*, TV program transcript, Ontario Educational Communications Authority)

The above excerpt is from the introductory segment of a recent television series designed to inform viewers about the future of work in our society. Like similar programs produced in other countries, this program presents a particular idea of "the future" with the intent of influencing how we think about and prepare ourselves for the years ahead. This kind of program represents what we will refer to as "the use of the future in the present." This notion is the theme that organizes the activities contained in this chapter. What we intend is a critical study of this theme. "The future" is not a destination, a place where we will eventually end up. It is a contestable vision, a particular human judgment, which can either incite change or justify existing realities. For students to be able to increase their effective participation in the determination of practices that define their working lives, they must be able to understand, assess, and, when necessary, contest prevailing images of the future.

The practice of using the future in the present is commonplace in the media but is also found in schools and homes when teachers and parents warn students about the need to prepare for the times ahead. Government policies are often also justified by appealing to visions of the future. How many times have we heard, for example, "the future of a country lies in the skills of its people?" And how many times have we been warned that unless we are prepared to invest in our human resources, Canada as a nation will find itself "out of the race?"

One image of the future that has been prominent in recent years is the vision of a new post-industrial society based on the promise that new technology will deliver interesting, complex, and diverse forms of future work. For post-industrial prophets, such visions require immediate investments in people to prepare for the realities to come. While there is little doubt that the adoption of computers and microchip technology will change the way many people work, to claim such changes will provide a new era of fulfilling jobs requires some critical assessment. More often than not, as new technology is introduced, work is being de-skilled, made more routine and less creative.

Talk of a second industrial revolution therefore might be premature. The idea that we are living through a process whereby the old industrial society is being transformed into one that is entirely new—that is, post-industrial, with new work, new lifestyles, and new values—suffers from a form of technological determinism that chooses to ignore the human context of such large-scale social change. Dream or nightmare, this vision of the future is presented as a fait accompli. Failure to adapt collectively to the imminent high-tech future, it is claimed, will result in entire nations being left behind in the competitive international marketplace. Failure to adapt individually will leave one functionally irrelevant in the "information age."

Post-industrial prophets implore people to prepare themselves for change, to learn to cope, to adjust to the future in a way that assumes public acquiescence to their grand technological design. Indeed, anyone who expresses misgivings about the progress which is the promise of high-technology is likely to be dismissed as nostalgic, computerphobic, or a Luddite. The challenges to any such grand design should not be so easily dismissed. Calls for changes in existing economic and cultural practices are commonly justified with reference to images of the future. If we are to participate in the determination of such changes, we must be able to assess the desirability of the possibilities in the images available to us.

The activities contained in this chapter are designed to support a questioning orientation toward images of the future. They start from our assumption that the use of images of the future is a form of social practice, a particular expression of possibilities always produced by someone for someone else and offered in very specific circumstances and with definite intended effects. Given this assumption, each activity encourages students to think about the relationship between the future and the present.

The following activities are contained in this chapter:

- Activity One: Talk about the future as a social practice
- Activity Two: Exploring responses to media presentations about the future
- Activity Three: Inquiring into current scenarios of the future
- Activity Four: Defining a desirable future

Activity One: Talk about the Future as a Social Practice

This activity is intended as an introduction to the idea of critically examining the use of images of the future as a social practice. This should be understood as an attempt to help students see how the idea of the future is often inserted into people's lives in an effort to bring about definite effects in the present. All students have probably engaged in some discussion about the future with parents and/or friends. Such discussions quite often include explicit or implicit expectations and desires about future possibilities. This activity begins by *working on* such experiences.

What to Do in the Classroom

Since the four activities listed in this chapter are interrelated and this is intended as an initial and introductory activity, introduce briefly the idea of the critical study of the use of the future in the present. Then introduce Activity One as the beginning of exploration of this topic.

On either chart paper or the board, write the following as headings of four columns:

- situations in which the future/your future was the topic of conversation
- who initiated this situation
- what images of the future were assumed
- what feelings you had about the conversation

After gathering a range of responses that describe a variety of situations, have students discuss the following: Which were the most pleasurable conversations? Contrast these with conversations that made students feel uncomfortable or bored. For these situations see if the students can characterize how specific versions of "the future" were being used in conversation.

Teaching Note

This activity is based on the assumption that students will have experienced different versions of the use of the future in their everyday lives. On the one hand are the uses of the future intended to get students to "listen up," that is, to take seriously some set of responsibilities or attitudes assumed essential for their own well-being. On the other hand, many students develop life projects by sharing their dreams and desires with friends or relatives. What is basic here is that all students will most likely have experienced specific uses of the future in the present and the particular consequences of such usage. It should be remembered that the purpose of this brief introductory activity is to simply introduce students to the core idea of this chapter: that the future is not a destination, but a contestable vision, a particular human judgment, that can either incite change or justify existing realities.

Activity Two: Exploring Responses to Media Presentations about the Future

Fascination with the future is nothing new. Speculating about the shape of things to come and warnings of the implications for the present have been recurrent themes of much television journalism and educational TV and film production. Examples of such programming are widely available not only in Canada but throughout the industrialized English-speaking world. Regardless of the country of origin, such productions seem to share a use of the future in the present that is analogous to the sounding of an alarm. The following activity begins with a ten-part TV Ontario series entitled "The Future of Work," which is typical of much of this kind of programming.

In promotional material, the TV Ontario series is described as having a two-part goal:

One, it will attempt to share with our viewers a picture, accurate as possible, of the work environment in the year 2000 and two, to offer them as many strategies as are available to best prepare for it. For both the visions and the strategies, we have called upon the best minds that were available to us from the fields of economics, business management, government, job forecasting and counselling, labor, industry and experts in high-technology (*Future Work Special*, TV Ontario)

The ten programs in the series deal with the following topics:

• productivity and technology
• new perceptions of work
• the office of the future

- industry in the future
- jobs of the future
- retraining
- small business
- the Ontario Paper Company
- reflections on the future
- learning a living in Canada

There is also a one-hour version of the series called *Future Work Special* which is particularly good for classroom use.

What to Do in the Classroom

The first step in this activity is to have the class view *Future Work Special* (or some suitable alternative). Such programs raise many important questions about work in the future. However, they should not be taken at face value. There is the need to critically examine the point of view being offered in such media constructions and that is the intention of the rest of this activity.

Teaching Note

We have taken the position throughout this book that work education should not be limited to discussion of how occupational mobility might be enhanced. As we have said in the introduction, to do so would be only to pit people against each other instead of encouraging collective strategies to address shared problems. The individualistic approach put forward in Future Work Special *in our view seriously undermines the effectiveness of this and other such programs for generating thought, discussion, and actions that would be the beginning of formulating solutions to the problems of organizing work in the future. Further steps in this activity will seek to clarify the limited character of such films.*

Distribute to the class the following statement, which is the response of Derek to advice given by workers in a work placement used by his high school cooperative education program. The issues raised here relate directly to the major concerns of the film.

Since I was a kid I've enjoyed working with my hands, taking things apart and fixing them. My dad, my brothers and I used to buy old cars and fix them up and sell them. What I'd like to do when I finish high school is go into machining and become a tool and die maker. A lot of people are talking about changes happening in work, eh. I know this one place where they had special machines—all computerized—like, I guess you have to have a lot of brains and a lot of experience for this type of work. All the machines run by remote control. They do everything, you know . . . drilling, tapping, reaming . . . like they say, in the future that's what it is all going to be about. It's going to be all digital readouts and remote control lathes . . . and it's going to be all different types of machines. Right now there is only a few people who know how to work that kind of machinery.

The guys where I'm doing my work experience say that I should go into something like computer programming, something where there is digital readouts and all that. And I don't know, I just want to get into tool and die. I think there will always be work. I want to be able to take a die apart and then if there is something that needs to be made, you know, I'll be able to make it, right? With the computers it's just not the same.

Ask students to consider how the information in the film might be relevant to their own plans for the future. Then discuss with the class how their individual responses compare with Derek's thoughts about his future at work.

Teaching Note

It will be important to listen carefully to the way students comprehend and deal with the messages of the film. The class discussion will be an opportunity to observe how students make sense of a specific incidence of the use of the future in the present. It is likely that some students will resist or dismiss the concerns of the film. Others will find themselves in agreement.

In addition, members of the class may display considerable disagreement with each other. Some students may judge those who reject the messages of the film as "romantics" or "technophobes," while those who embrace it may be seen as "computer freaks" or "technophiles." What must be constantly clear in the discussion is that the people whose lives are affected by technology have a legitimate concern and interest in determining how that technology will be implemented. Moreover, characterizing people as either "romantic Luddites" or "computer freaks" suppresses necessary consideration of value questions and denigrates legitimate struggles over such issues.

By this point in this activity students should have a clear idea of how the film is a specific example of an attempt to use the future in the present. The members of the class will have discovered that the film can have real effects on how people think about their possible futures and how they feel about their preparedness and capabilities to survive and "make it" in "the information age." However, students must not be left with a naive, uncritical view of such media productions. What needs to be made explicit are the ways in which the apparent authority of the film is constructed. The following is a suggested procedure for raising such issues.

1. Make it clear that it is now time to "review" the film in order to trace how it was put together as a particular image of the future. Show the film once again, asking students to take notes on the various features of the film they think are central to the construction of its point of view. Suggestions would be to note the use of voice over narration, music, juxtaposition of images, camera angles, background sets for interview segments, and so on.

2. Individually, in groups, or with the whole class, ask students to develop a statement of the dominant point of view of the film and a list of all the production techniques that organize the presentation of this point of view. Then have students consider the following: Whose point of view is this? Whose interests are served by this point of view and whose are diminished? What questions are asked within this point of view and what questions are left out? Are there other points of view presented? Whose points of view are not represented?

3. Media productions like this film do not simply appear in schools. As all teachers know, the availability of materials for classroom use is often related to the issue of point of view. Some points of view are more available than others. Discuss with the class the ease or difficulty you have had in obtaining the film you have used. Together with the class set yourselves the task of finding other media productions with different points of view. In the process, see if you can determine some of the factors that influence how and why some media and print resources are more available for class use than others. What are the implications of this for making students aware of a variety of points of view about work?

Teaching Note

It is important that this review of the film not be seen as simply an academic exercise. In naming and interrogating the implications of a particular point of view, students are opening up the question of how information about the future is produced, who is producing it and why, what range of information they are being given access to, and what they would have to do to be better informed. These are issues that connect directly to the next activity and it is crucial that the teacher make clear the connection between this activity and the next.

Activity Three: Inquiring into Current Scenarios of the Future

As the previous activity has shown, most material available for use in classrooms presents common, widely held views of the future. There are, however, other possibilities. The following activity is designed to encourage students to broaden the scope of their thinking about the future of work.

Among the factors futurists consider when generating scenarios about work are: the technological growth rate; the economic growth rate; the quality of jobs generated; and the distribution of work and income. Martin Morf (1983) uses these factors to create eight scenarios of what work might be like in the future.[1] Morf develops his typology along three lines. Four of the scenarios presume more technology and less work; three presume more technology and more work; and the final scenario presumes a less technologized future.

The following four scenarios are based on the widely accepted assumption that the rate of growth of technology will continue, bringing with it a reduction in the number of available jobs.

Scenario 1: Extreme Taylorism

Under this scenario, work has been so rationalized that machines, computers, and robots produce most of the goods and services consumed by the society. In this "leisure society," work is superfluous and a basic income can be earned by working a few hours a day or a day or two a week. Liberated by high-tech, individuals in this society of the future "work less and live more"; that is, they spend more of their time doing what they want rather than working for what they need.

Scenario 2: Feudal Unions

The prospect of less work raises the question of how available work and income are distributed throughout the society. While work and income are presumed to be evenly distributed in the "leisure society," in this scenario powerful unions distribute work by controlling access to jobs. These "feudal unions" not only defend their members against employers and technology, but also resist encroachment by the unorganized work force.

Scenario 3: Underground Work

Less work could mean more and more workers being forced out of the formal economy. High-tech jobs requiring high-tech credentials could put high-paying and secure jobs out of reach of most workers in society. If feudal unions control access to the rest of the available work, the jobless are left to fend for themselves in the informal economy.

Scenario 4: Work Coupons

The problem of distributing jobs in a society where income is still contingent upon having paid employment is ameliorated if jobs can be rationed. In this scenario, "work coupons" are seen as providing an equitable means of distributing jobs.

It is sometimes claimed that new technology creates as many jobs as it eliminates by developing new products and the need for new services. The following three scenarios are based on the proposition that more technology means more work.

Scenario 5: Gods and Clods

If the new technology is inaccessible to the majority of the population, the work force could develop into a small, fully employed, well-paid, technological elite and a large, poorly paid, techno-peasantry.

Scenario 6: Shadow Work

Because the productive, wealth-generating work is done by the technological elite, most workers are engaged in "shadow work," that is, work that is unnecessary and caters to artificially created personal needs.

Scenario 7: The Electronic Cottage

In this scenario new technology is highly pervasive and accessible to all. High productivity and economic growth combine to create sufficient work that is fairly distributed among the working population.

The final scenario challenges the basic assumption of all the others: that the rate of technological growth will continue to increase.

Scenario 8: Subsistence Work

This scenario suggests that technological growth might be constrained by natural resource limitations. Society, in this view, must learn to lower expectations of ever-increasing material goods. Quality of life would improve as people recognize the limitations of what the economy can provide and adjust their needs and wants accordingly.

What to Do in the Classroom

Have students read "Eight Scenarios for Work in the Future" by Martin Morf or present the material in class. Discuss and clarify each scenario. Have students consider which versions correspond to their taken-for-granted images of the future and which versions are ones they have never considered.

Students are now in a position to begin exploring the range of available visions of the future that might correspond to the broad spectrum of possibilities outlined in the eight scenarios. The following activity proceeds over a period of time and requires the allocation of classroom space for semi-permanent displays. Set aside a large classroom space on either walls, movable panels, or charts. Within this space, label a clearly defined area for each of the above scenarios. This space will then be used to display information about the future of work students bring to class. This might be done through the following procedure.

1. Have students collect or reproduce images about the future of work that appear in newspapers, television, magazines, books, and films.

2. Using Morf's typology have students determine which scenario or combination of scenarios these images represent. In order to do this students must consider the basic assumptions made with regard to: the rate of technological growth, the rate of economic growth, the quality of jobs created in the future, and the distribution of work and income. When a determination is made have students post the information and images in the appropriate display spaces.

3. This process of collection and display of information and images should go on for a reasonable length of time to allow students to discover a range of ideas being presented. From time to time, it will be important to note and discuss with the class what display spaces contain the most information and what spaces contain the least. If material seems to be scarce in a few panels students might be assigned specifically to find information pertinent to the relevant scenarios.

4. To conclude this activity, discuss with students the results of their research. Without question, information will be easier to locate for some of the scenarios than others. Have the class consider why this may be so and what the implications of this are. Furthermore, since none of these images of the future are neutral—they all presume specific beneficiaries and casualties—the question of who stands to benefit most from each scenario should be considered.

Teaching Note

The categories in Morf's scheme are not exclusive and thus the placement of some information brought to class by students may be open to interpretation. Furthermore, if the class thinks that new scenarios should be generated to better describe information that is collected, display spaces can be added as required.

Activity Four: Defining a Desirable Future

To this point in this chapter, students have been asked to consider a variety of possible scenarios for the future defined by people other than themselves. As has been stressed, such an activity is not just a matter of prediction; it is also a question of value, a question of the direction in which we should desire. In this concluding activity of the chapter, students are given an opportunity to formulate their own notions of a desirable future and to consider what would have to be done for such futures to come about. The activity is presented last in this chapter as it assumes some knowledge about the process of developing possible scenarios of the future.

What to Do in the Classroom

Divide the class into groups and assign each group the task of defining a plausible and desirable scenario for society 25 years from now. This may be structured for students, by asking them to make clear their assumptions and preferences in regard to the four factors that were the focus of study in Activity Three: the technological growth rate, the economic growth rate, the quality of jobs generated, and the distribution of work and income. Have each group outline key aspects of its vision of the future on chart paper.

Post each of these scenarios in front of the entire class and discuss what actions would have to be taken and what changes would have to be accomplished in order for each scenario to be realized. List the relevant actions next to each scenario.

Based on their assessments of the likelihood of such actions and changes, have members of the class rank each scenario in terms of how possible each seems. Have class members share their rankings. Using differences among the rankings as a starting point, identify different assumptions students have about the possibility of certain actions and changes.

The different assumptions students identify in the preceding steps will often comprise a variety of assertions about the notion of human nature as well as disagreements over the inevitability of certain attitudes and behaviors. Such disagreements should be highlighted as areas for future study and consideration. Students should be challenged to consider how their own assertions of their assumptions are grounded and how they would go about further testing these assumptions. A deeper consideration of the contentiousness of these assumptions might form the basis of individual assignments.

NOTE

1. Martin Morf. "Eight Scenarios for Work in the Future," *The Futurist*, June 1983, pp. 24–29.

Index

audit, health and safety, 101–4
authority, 83–85

benefits, 170
Braverman, Harry, 55–56

Canadian Classification and
  Dictionary of Occupations (CCDO),
  157
Canadian Co-operative Association,
  40
collective action, 129–32
cultural politics: and pedagogy, 4;
  and teaching strategy, 14–15, 98

Dewey, John, 5
domestic life, its relation to paid
  work, 113–14, 119–21

exchange relations, 7, 171–72, 175
experience: interviewing and, 20–21;
  journal-writing and, 18–19;
  reflective learning and, 13–14; as
  socially accomplished, 9–10;
  teaching strategy and, 17–20;
  working "on" and working

"with," 10–12, 18, 20–21, 83, 99–
  101, 114, 119, 133, 187–88

Ford, Henry, 49–50
Future Work (Ontario Educational
  Communications Authority), 185,
  188

gender: authority and, 85; culture of
  work and, 35, 78–80, 107; division
  of labor and, 49 (*see also* domestic
  life); the double day, 119–20; pay
  equity and, 173–74; sexual
  harassment, 91

Industrial Accident Prevention
  Association (IAPA), 105, 112–13
initiative, 38, 62–65, 69, 81–83
interviewing as strategy for:
  assessing job descriptions, 163;
  clarifying job "choices," 157–58,
  163; investigating workplace
  changes, 52; learning from others,
  20–21, 118–19, 124–25, 133–35;
  understanding workers' response
  to work, 159–61

job competence, 27–29, 42–43, 46, 58
job descriptions: role in shaping the
notion of "skill," 47–49; and self-
assessment, 162–63
job interviews, 177–79; rights in, 179–
81; role playing for, 178–79
job satisfaction: facing trade offs,
115–16, 122–25; understanding the
view of others, 114–19
job search strategies, 181–83
journal-writing: as inquiry into
"working knowledge," 34–38; and
self-assessment, 158–59; as
strategy, 18–19

Lavigne, Merve, 138–45
Leffingwell, Henry, 49–52
leisure, its relation to work, 113–14,
121–22

monitoring, of students at worksite,
65, 70–72
Moore, David, and pedagogy of
work experience, 58–65
Morf, Martin, 191–94, 195

National Citizens Coalition (NCC),
139–40, 141–45

occupational health and safety:
allocating responsibility for solving
problems, 96, 104–5; collective
responsibility for, 97, 110–12;
defining a health and safety
problem, 96, 98–104; and the social
context of work, 96, 105–10
Ontario Public Service Employees
Union (OPSEU), 138–45

pay: fairness of, 171–72; methods of,
167–68; quality of, 168–70
pay equity, 173–74
photography, as critical reflection on
"working knowledge," 32–33

Rand formula, 141, 144, 145–46
reflective learning, 13–14
resumes, 175–77

role play, 110, 160, 178–79
Rubin, Lillian, 124

Sayer, Liz, 154–55
schooling: as cultural politics, 4, 9;
policy and relation to the economy,
4–9
self-assessment: definitions of, 150–
52; life changes and, 152–54;
vocational testing, 154–58
sexual harassment, 85, 91
skill: job descriptions, 48–49;
"production of" versus "individual
ability," 45–46; social differences
and, 54–55; workplace changes
and, 52; work rationalization, 49–54
Snedden, David, 5–6
social relations, 7; authority and, 83–
85; conventions and routines, 78–
81; initiative and, 81–83; viewpoint
for understanding, 76–78; work
identities and, 85–86
student evaluation, 65, 69–70, 72
student training profiles, 65–70
Swail, Audrey, 154–55

teaching strategy: definition of, 14–
15; cultural politics and, 15;
technique and, 14–15, 17, 20; as
means of contextualizing
curriculum, 22–23; in relation to
group discussion, 30, 34–36, 38,
134–35, 137
technical relations, 7
Terkel, Studs, *Working*, 159

unions: as a form of collective action,
127–28, 132–35; and labor history,
135–38; and labor law, 138–45

vocational testing, benefits and
limits, 154–58

White, Justice John, 139, 143–45
work education, contemporary
approaches to, 6–8
work futures: alternative scenarios of,
191–94; conceptions of, 185–88;

desirable futures, 194–95; media presentations of, 188–91

work identities, 85–86

work rationalization, 49–54

work refusal, 108–10, 172

worker cooperatives, and working knowledge, 39–42

Workers' Health and Safety Centre, 105, 111

working collectively: in relation to group discussion, 30, 35–36; as strategy, 15–17

working knowledge: activities for introducing the notion of, 31–34; and agency, 42–43; alternative forms of worker cooperatives, 38–42; gaining access to, 34–38; "production of" versus "acquisition," 30; types of, 28

ABOUT THE AUTHORS

ROGER I. SIMON teaches in the Department of Curriculum at the Ontario Institute for Studies in Education. He was co-director of Project Learning Work, an extensive multi-year ethnographic study of student experiences in work education programs. Simon has conducted research and written extensively in the areas of critical pedagogy and cultural studies, work that has emphasized theoretical and applied frameworks. He is currently completing his next book *Teaching against the Grain: Essays for a Pedagogy of Possibility*.

DON DIPPO teaches on the Faculty of Education at York University. His research interests include the social and political organization of knowledge, critical pedagogy and cultural studies, and the sociology of work and occupations.

ARLEEN SCHENKE is presently doing graduate work in Sociology at the Ontario Institute for Studies in Education. Having taught at the secondary school and community college levels, she is currently an instructor at the School of Continuing Studies, University of Toronto, and a teaching assistant at York University's Faculty of Education. Her research interests focus on feminist and post-structuralist applications to the practice of critical pedagogy and cultural studies.